Be the Joy of God

Be the Joy of God

Ankit Kumar

ISBN: 978-93-5128-236-5

Price: ₹ 150

First Published, 2017

Published by

Kalpaz Publications
C-30, Satyawati Nagar,
Delhi – 110052
E-mail: kalpaz@hotmail.com
Ph.: 9212142040

Printed at: G. Print Process, Delhi

Cataloging in Publication Data—DK
Courtesy: D.K. Agencies (P) Ltd. <docinfo@dkagencies.com>

Kumar, Ankit *(IT consultant)*, **author.**
Be the joy of God / Ankit Kumar.
pages cm
Includes bibliographical references.
ISBN 9789351282365

1. God—Love—Anecdotes. 2. College students—Religious life—Anecdotes. 3. Kumar, Ankit (IT consultant)—Anecdotes. 4. Kumar, Ankit (IT consultant)—Friends and associates—Anecdotes. I. Title.

BL626.35.K86 2016 DDC 212.7 23

Contents

Preface

'Joy of God' is a philosophical conception, exploring the ideas and methods which could help each one of us to be the source of Almighty's smiles! Be the 'Joy of God'. We all could become the source of God's Joy! Each day and every moment we all could aspire to live in such a way that when God looks at us, God smiles! It would lead to a beautiful world around us as well as revamp our personal development and growth.

The Story unfolds when four college friends get together in an alumni meet. While discussing about their lives situations, they end up learning about *being the source of Almighty's smiles, being the 'Joy of God'*.

These ideas are simple and can be incorporated in our daily lives. The ideas and methods give us another perspective in our lives. They inspire us to lead a lifestyle where we care about being the Joy to God; where we care about making our Mother Earth more beautiful, loving and peaceful every moment.

Aspire to be the 'Joy of God'. The transition would also help us to feel the love, care and protection of God in our lives. This shall help us to reconnect with our creator and bring God's Love in our lives. God would become our guide and friend.

Remember that the vision is important. The ideas discussed in this book are not exhaustive. It is my humble effort to pen down few ideas. Vision is required to follow a path. The path could be yours; the idea and method to be 'Joy of God' could be yours! Follow your heart, the light is within!

May, you be the 'Joy of God'.

Acknowledgements

First and foremost, I would thank the almighty, God. Thank you for being there with me through my thick and thin times. Thank you for giving me the gift of 'writing'. I bow down to you in gratitude.

I thank my father, Mr Subhendu Sahay, my mother, Mrs Anita Sahay and my sister, Nimisha for being there in my life. Their mere presence brings joy in my life. Thank you Akhilesh Sir, my teacher, for instilling confidence in me. I need to thank my parents and my maternal grand-father, Late Shri Dina Nath Sharan, for showing me how to 'give back' good to society. Children learn what they see around them. Thank you!

Many thanks to my friends for loving my poetry and writing, and encouraging me to bring them out in the world.Thank you Aayush Kumar, Aanal Kumar, Amisha Chauhan, Puneeth K, Ujjwal Gupta, Parul Mago, Rohit Chopra, Sudha Bhat, Chetan Sahu, Bhaskar, Deepshikha Singh, Abdul Aziz, Abhishek, Aashish, Ansuman Nayak, Rajendra Alluri, Mrinal Kumar. It was your love and support at one point or the other that I am, who I am! All I want to say is: Thank you. Thank you for having crossed your path with mine. You have made my life beautiful!

Special thanks to Aayush Kumar for the endless discussions we have had on how to give back good to society and instead of complaining, going out and making a difference. Thanks for your valuable inputs and reviews of this book.

I am very grateful to my publisher and editor for sharing my zeal on the 'joy of god' conception, and helping me to spread the message through this book.

May, you be the 'Joy of God'.

— **Ankit Kumar**

Chapter - I

May, You be the Joy of God!

It was the summer of 2016. I was cheerfully strolling in my alma mater's campus garden rejoicing some beautiful moments of my college days, rekindling some deep emotions. Every year my college, Manipal Institute of Technology organises an Alumni meet for the batch which graduated five years back, to celebrate their success and to make them guide the next batch for the placements, helping them understand the world outside the walls of our beloved college.

I was there in Manipal, at the Alumni meet. I was hopeful to finally meet my dearest mates – Sarika, Ayush and Surbhit, after a long time. It's been five years since we graduated, yet we hardly ever met! Everyone got so busy in their lives and career that we four never ended up being together at same place. Three of us worked in different locations in our country, and one worked in a different time zone. Whenever we planned a get-together, one or the other always could not make it. It was the alumni meet that we four finally decided to get together.

As I entered my college canteen, I could hear the loud giggles of Sarika. She had a trademark laugh, one which could make her entourage burst out laughing even more. I saw my three besties and in a moment we four were in a big hug. Emotions were on roll. Even my nerdy friend, Ayush had a drop of tear in his eyes. Sarika, Surbhit and I were humbled by the emotions as well.

* * *

The cafeteria was still buzzing with students as it used to be. We ordered tea and snacks, and sat around a table with smiles on our faces. We felt like college kids again, for one more time. We were having a round of know-how about each other's lives, when Sarika took a sip of her green tea and asked me,

"So Amrit, you have started exercising I guess. You look so fit and lean." Everyone had another burst of laughter. They remembered how I was in my college days with the round tummy bursting out of the t-shirts.

"Well, in short, life has been good and inspiring in last couple of years", I said.

My London-settled friend who was pursuing masters in water science, Ayush said, "Yes brother, you have changed a lot. Good for you."

"Good to see you happy, Amrit. Is this transformation some how related to the *Bodh Gaya* trip you had mentioned in your emails?"probably Surbhit felt some connection and quickly asked me.

"Yes Amrit. Tell us about that trip. You were so eager. In your emails you had mentioned that the trip gave you another perspective to look at life and transformed your lifestyle!" seconded Sarika.

I replied with a smile, "You are right on the money Surbhit. Sarika, it is indeed the truth. The Bodh Gaya trip has brought wonders in my life. You are my closest friends, there is no point hiding from you guys. I had good education and then a cool and high paying job. I used to pack my bag every now and then, and travel, visit new places, see and cherish the beauty of nature. Yet, something was still missing. It's hard to explain. It's like there was avoid in my heart, which was never getting filled no matter what I did. Rather I would say, there was a sense of hollowness inside me.

The heart was urging for something which I was not able to discover. The more the 'void' remained unfulfilled, the more emptiness I felt. A sense of sadness started prevailing in my life, no matter what I did! Then the Bodh Gaya trip came in my life, which brought wonders. I feel more happy, content and peaceful now".

"Dude, you got to share your views with us. These days I have been grumping a lot. I never feel satisfied and happy with my job or life!", said Ayush.

I seconded, "I understand Ayush. Even I used to feel the same. I used to feel that life was so un-fruitful. In time, it brought too much bitterness and anger with it too!"

"Then why did you keep this thing, this idea inside you for so long. Why didn't you share with us earlier? Haven't you heard an old saying that knowledge spreads only by sharing with others!" Sarika burst out at me complaining.

She was angry at me but somehow that brought smile on my face. I waited a couple of seconds to let the storm settle down. "I wanted to meet you guys in person and talk about it, discuss the idea in person. But, we four could never meet together since our college farewell. Even I wanted to share this idea, this wisdom or knowledge with you guys. And for days, I have been eagerly waiting for our alumni meet so that we all could meet together." Sarika's anger gave way to a hint of smile.

"Sorry mate. But we all are here now. I think that life wanted to give us some time to face hardships, to experience the outside world first so that we get ready to understand the life wisdom you talk about!", said Ayush thoughtfully.

"So true Ayush. I used to feel that I was going nowhere. Life became very mundane. I started becoming unsure of myself or of my decisions. I was just walking down on a dark path and I couldn't see where it led me.

But, God had plans for me! Somehow I ended up visiting Bodh Gaya and it completely changed my perspective of life. So, let me tell you about it", I said.

* * *

"My career graph started going downhill. I had no plans for post-graduation. I even had a break up with the love of my life. I felt like I was heading for a ditch. Nothing was falling in place. These thoughts played a lot with my mind. So I decided to take two weeks break from my life and went home, Patna.

You know, I had never visited Bodh Gaya before, it being just a hundred kilometers away from Patna. I had spent my whole childhood in Patna but I never visited the holy place before."

"But how did you end up in Bodh Gaya? I had never seen you visiting a temple in your four years of college life!" asked Sarika.

"Well, these thoughts were firmly held in my head. I was desperate to do something, for a change. I guess, I had witnessed the 'low' of my life. As Ayush said earlier, I think that life was making me ready for a life lesson. God had planned it all perfectly.

Amazingly, on the second day of my vacation I won a lottery in shopping mall which entitled me to a three-day package tour to Bodh Gaya!"

"Wow man! You won a lottery trip! You were lost and life gave you a surprise. Interesting."Ayush gently punched his fist on my shoulders.

"Yes. I second that. It's called the 'Cycle of time' about which I learnt in Bodh Gaya", I said.

* * *

I continued, "In Bodh Gaya, as my tour bus stopped at the Bodhi temple I felt as if something was attracting me, like a magnet. It was strange, unexplainable feeling. I felt that I belonged! I felt that life had brought me here for a purpose. Like there was a hidden treasure to be unraveled.

Following my instincts and the guide, I went to the temple, strolled around it and at last I found myself standing in front of the 'Bodhi Tree' under which Lord Buddha had gained enlightenment.

I don't know how, but I felt very peaceful and serene being there. I was feeling complete and happy. I had grown alien to these feelings, yet they soothed me. I felt at home, like surrounded by the love of my parents and family. In a matter of second, feelings of anger, depression and loneliness had faded away. My heart was filled with love. There was no void anymore!

Then I saw a saint signalling in my direction. I turned around to see whom the saint was calling, but there was no one behind me. It was me. I walked towards him.

The saint said, "Son, somehow I noticed you when you were around this sacred 'Bodhi tree'. I can see in your eyes the happiness and content which you are feeling now."

"Yes sir, this place has a magical effect. I was very remorse and sad when I came here. But, this place, this sacred tree has somehow made me serene", I said.

"You felt the love of God around you, son. The mere presence of God's love does that to one's heart. It makes you feel complete. *It's just that people fail to see this love every day and around them!*" said the enlightened saint.

Seeing my perplexed face, the saint kept his hand on my head and said with a hint of smile, '*May, you be the Joy of God!*'

* * *

Sarika exclaimed, "Be the 'Joy of God'! What does that even mean?"

I replied with a smile on my face, "Well, seeing my perplexed face again, the saint explained,

We all should aspire to be the source of God's joy, be the 'Joy of God'. We should live such that when God looks at us, God smiles! And when we just do that, our world opens up to embrace God and fills our heart with his Love!"

"Wow! That's such a simple definition to such a noble idea", Ayush said joyfully.

Surbhit rose from his thoughts, feeling stirred and asked, "But why?Why should I care about being the 'Joy of God'? What can it do to me? Amrit, you were like an atheist in college days, and now you are talking about God! I just want to lead a normal, simple and day-to-day life. Why should I follow this philosophical way of life? Can it help me?"

"Believe me Surbhit, I had the same questions and thoughts as you are having now. The saint smiled at my inquisition and explained me how the noble idea could do wonders for the world, the people around us and enhance our life as a whole!"

Sarika affirmed, "You look very happy and content in life Amrit. I will buy that. I mean, I can clearly see the transformation in you in just a single year! May be I will also incorporate this new lifestyle. Please tell us more about this noble idea of being the 'Joy of God'."

"Why not Sarika. I had been eager to meet you guys so that I could share the idea with you all.

This idea shall teach us, take us on a journey and show us why it is important to be the 'Joy of God'! It would teach us how by doing simple things which could make us the 'Joy of God', in turn also impacts and changes our lives spiritually.

Firstly, by performing the ideas and methods as described by the saint we would bring joy to our creator, the Almighty; God.

Secondly, this path would enrich our lives us as well. We would feel good about ourself, bring peace and calmness to our heart, and know what is right and what is wrong morally or socially in a situation. We would feel the love and blessing of God in our life. It would help us to fight our frustration, anger or loneliness."

Ayush asked, "But what if the ideas and methods don't appeal to me? Do I need to necessarily follow the Saint's methods?"

I said after some thought, "At least give it a try. Remember that the 'Joy of God' vision is enlightening. The ideas discussed further are not exhaustive. Vision is required to follow a path. The path could be yours; the idea and method to be 'Joy of God' could be yours! Follow your heart, the light is within!"

"These ideas and methods described by the saint would help us to bring smiles to God and makes us the 'Joy of God'. It would make us happy doing 'God's work'. This path has too much in store for us. Let's explore", I affirmed feeling possessed by the noble idea.

* * *

Surbhit questioned, "Who all can implement these ideas? I have my MBA classes in a couple of months. Keeping in mind the time and energy I have to spend in my MBA, if I spend some time and energy on these ideas, will it help me? Or will I be wasting my resources?"

"Wow man, you already have a manager mind. Thinking about resource allocations from now itself", giggled Sarika.We all burst out laughing.

Holding my laughter, I confirmed Surbhit, "This is for you, for me and for everyone around us. But you don't need to believe because I say so. Just practice it yourself for couple of months and believe what you feel, believe what you experience out of it. Give it a try atleast.

As far as time and efforts go, the best thing is that it's a lifestyle whose ideas and methods could be incorporated in our day-to-day life. It's practical. Experiment and see the results yourself! This lifestyle would transform you. This lifestyle is for each and every one of us."

"How can it impact people's lives Amrit?" said thoughtful Ayush.

"In today's world many of us are surrounded by depression, some are frustrated with life, some have too much agony inside and some feel lonely. On one side there is unhappiness and on the other there is dissatisfaction with life, career, love, or friends. We see ourselves surrounded by miseries and sometimes all paths seem to flow towards emptiness. Sometimes we just feel that we are walking down a road, not living it. Not living the life!

The 'Joy of God' lifestyle gives each one of us an opportunity to make our lives more beautiful! That's how 'Joy of God' ideas could transform each and every one of us."

'May, you be the Joy of God'

* * *

Chapter - II

Expectations and Misery

It was evening and the college classes would have dispersed. The cafeteria was now buzzing with students. Sarika was in some deep thought. I inquired, "What's the matter Sarika? What are you thinking about?"

"You know Amrit, sometimes I think that *we focus so much on 'one' thing that we fail to see many 'ones' manifest! And that leads to misery.*" felt Sarika.

"Amazing perspective Sarika. Well, that reminds of what the saint told me,

'Expect less and enjoy small things more'.

He said that we humans have a fragile heart which easily gets swayed into sadness or joy. We always expect more and more, and many a times, these 'expectations' are the greatest reason of our sorrows. No matter what life bestows us, we just tend to look at the shortcomings and what we didn't get. We are not able to enjoy small joys of life because we expect more!

Build your talent, build yourself and enhance your reality. But keep the expectation in check. The saint had beautifully summarised this in a mathematical way,

'*Happiness = Reality – Expectations*'.

We get angry at people and life because we expect more. We get swayed by sadness or anger when someone does not rises up to our 'own' expectations! We have too many expectations, which are killing the joy in our lives daily and each moment. We expect more because we tend to 'want' more, more than what we 'need'! There is a thin line difference between a need and a want.

The saint told that, *'Need' is something you have to have, whereas 'want' is something you would like to have.*

The day we understand our 'need' and separate it from our 'wants', life would be much simpler, easy, less stressful and fun to live."

"Wow man, the saint was truly an enlightened soul" conferred Ayush. He continued, "I must give his ideas a try. The way I see it now, there is nothing to lose in this lifestyle. All I need to care about is the smiles on the face of my creator! Simple."

"I second that. Imagine, I ended up living for a week in Bodh Gaya just to interact with the holy saint daily. And it brought wonders in my life!" I affirmed joyously.

* * *

After some deep thought Surbhit said, "But, what exactly brings miseries in our lives? Why isn't life full of wonders always?"

"It's the 'cycle of time' Surbhit. Neither I nor you or anyone can control that. The Saint believed that life is a cycle of time; bad followed by good, followed by bad and then good again and so on. The cycle goes on. We will discuss more on this cycle of time later. Rather I would tell what the saint believed about miseries. The holy man said,

"*Our miseries are enhanced or subdued by the way we see our lives.*"

Like a coin has two sides, our life also has two sides, rather perspectives. It's upon us to decide which side we want to see. Miseries or dissatisfaction is there persistently because we are looking at the dimmer side of the coin consciously or sub-consciously, which enhances our fear or the impact of the misery. We need to change our perspective and outlook of situations and circumstances. We are expecting more and more, even before accepting and acknowledging what we already have!

We must learn to see the bright side of things and circumstances, recognise and thank for our fortunes and blessings. Our 'want' and expectations lead us to unhappiness, which makes us to look at dimmer-side of things and situations, every time. Just jot down your 'needs' and 'wants' in a paper. You will then see that God has given you much more than your 'needs'. Shouldn't this be a reason for you to be happy? Start looking at the brighter-side of things" I explained.

This intrigued Sarika, "But, why do we generally look the dimmer side of coin?"

"Sarika, it's like we are standing in a wind, face against it. Then we say that wind is blowing against us. All I want to say is just turn around; the wind wants to lead you somewhere. It's God's hand. Just look for another angle, another perspective at things and you would see bright side. The next time you feel unhappy or dissatisfied; just remind yourself to '*turn around*'.

Many a times we tend to think that whatever path we choose in life, it might lead to a pit, that we might be unsuccessful no matter what. We then lose confidence in ourselves. Even I used to think and feel the same a year back.

All these have happened because we have moved more and more away from our creator, spiritually. We have got various fears in our day-to-day life, as people now do not feel that they are protected by God. It's like the warmth and protection a child feels in a mother's love. God's Love will always be there in our lives, what's missing is our '*belief*' that God's Love exists in our lives! We need to teach ourselves to bring that 'belief' again in our lives. We need to connect again with our creator."

"Oh, that's why the holy saint told you that 'people fail to see the God's love every day' when you first met him under the Bodhi tree?" intrigued Ayush.

"Exactly Ayush. That's what the holy saint explained to me later. We have lost our touch, our connection with the Supreme God, our creator. This has aggravated our fears and agony as we don't feel warmth and protection of God. Remember, a human heart is always hungry for Love! What can be a better source of love than God, the never ending, enriching Love of God in our hearts!

The saint's ideas shall embark us on a journey to learn the ways to connect again with our creator and bring back joy, happiness and most importantly, love and peace in our hearts. Like a parent is filled with joy due to happiness of child, God shall be happy seeing you smile; and God shall smile back. For us to be the Joy of God, it's necessary to bring joy in our hearts, first."

Sarika put in her views on this. "I think, practically God's Love could help me this way. If I am unsure of my path, or afraid to take the risk, afraid of what might come at the end of this road; then I must remind myself that it's always better to go the extra mile and take the risk. It's much worth than regretting later in my life. I need not fear as I have love of God in my life each moment.Whatever the outcome be, I have my creator loving me and caring for me. With God by my side, the world is at my helms. I would 'believe' that and Go for it!"

"That's wonderfully explained Sarika. You have always been a bright student" I conferred.

Surbhit raises his concerns now. "Okay. So I get that in our modern times, most of us have moved away from our creator spiritually. And due to the lack of God's Love we start to feel the 'lack' of everything! Which gives birth to anger, bitterness, and loneliness and enhances our miseries. But, what I am still not able to grasp is *how do we feel this Love of God?"*

I had to explain my thoughts on this.

"Surbhit, we can feel the God's Love again in our lives. The connection between an individual's heart and God is a very personal relationship. Basically, God loves us nonetheless as we all are God's sons and daughters. But, it's we who feel detached. We need to feel that attachment and connection again with God. That's where this 'Joy of God' lifestyle is most helpful. This lifestyle shall teach us to be the 'Joy of God' and in return also help us to re-connect every moment with our creator. We would then feel God's Love, blessings and presence in our lives.

There are many methods practiced by the holy saint himself and his disciples, which could help us to feel God's Love in our life and be the joy of God. The saint's ideas like 'Morning Mirror test', 'giving back' and 'Gratitude' would help us to bring God close to our hearts. They teach us how to be the 'Joy of God'."

Sarika was again possessed by some deep thoughts on this and she said, "I am starting to get a feel of this lifestyle."

Ayush was eager to hear her interpretation. "Please share your thoughts on this Sarika."

"Basically, God smiles at us when we do God's work. Our life is showered with God's Love and blessings. We would start feeling the love and presence of God in our life. We will start 'believing' more in ourselves. We will be more and more grateful to and acknowledge our blessings. Wherever we would look, the sight of the beautiful world around us would bring more and more happiness to us. We would no more be unhappy or dissatisfied with life, career, love or friends.

Also, by being the 'Joy of God' we would bring 'Love of God' in our life, and this love fills up any sorrow, pain or misery we have had before! We would feel loved, cared for and protected by our creator.

The Love of God can transform us and our life. To start with, we will never feel lonely as God would always be there with us, in us. We would never feel emptiness inside, as we would know that God has showered love in our lives. We would never feel depressed or frustrated as we would acknowledge all the gifts God has given us, and we would be grateful! We would be at peace and happy. Our life would be transformed.

This transformation in us would make God happier. Firstly, we, the son or daughter of God, are happy. Hence seeing his/her child happy, God would be happy and smiling. Secondly, the work that we would do, 'God's work', a good Karma would make God happy. We would be the Joy of God!" exclaimed Sarika with a big smile on her face.

* * *

Ayush still had some doubts in his mind, "I have a friend who doesn't believes in existence of God. Sarika told earlier that knowledge can only spread if we share it. How do I then share and explain the 'Joy of God' idea to him?"

I must say, that was a tricky one. It left me wondering how I could explain the 'Joy of God' idea to someone who doesn't believes in God! I started speaking slowly, not sure how I was going to put it.

"It gives me a great satisfaction if I feel that there is a powerful force watching over me. That this supreme power loves me. A power, which has created this whole universe. A power, which has made life possible on our mother Earth. Providing the exact range of temperature for life to exist! Giving us the atmosphere to protect us and sustain life on earth, and many more miracles we see or hear about. A power, which is beyond our thoughts. Yet, we see them every day and in every moment!

This power, this force is God to me. The Divine Creator. Some call him 'Krishna'. Some call him 'Jesus'. Some 'Allah'. And some call it 'Science'. It could be a supreme intelligence guiding this universe. Some call it 'Mother Nature'. Name it whatever you want. The relation between a man and his creator is a very personal feeling. For simplicity, let's call it our 'Creator'. We cannot deny the magnificence and grandeur of our creator. We need this creator, God! A belief in God's existence and majestic power is what we all need.

We need God in despair to scream at. We need God to cry out our soul to. We need God to make us believe that someone more powerful is there for us. We also need God to thank for our successes and triumphs. We need to '*believe*' in the supreme power!

It shall be our belief that we will triumph as God is watching over us. The important thing is that we '*believe*'. And when we believe that there is God watching over us, we believe more in ourselves. It is very important to believe in God so that humanity can progress. We all are sons and daughters of the Almighty. And we, therefore, possess the powers too! We just need to 'believe'. God is present in each of us; in the rich person you see, in the barber, in the cleaner, even in the plants and animals.

God is everywhere. Everything has been created by our creator and is a part of him. We all living creatures are part of God's soul. We have God in our heart."

I finished this in a single breath, gasping for air now. During the explanation I felt as if our Creator guided me to explain why we need our creator!

* * *

I quickly glanced at my watch and it was already seven. We were getting late for the alumni meet dinner ceremony. I looked at Ayush, Surbhit and Sarika. All were in some deep thought. I felt content. At least I got them thinking of this lifestyle.

Sarika broke the silence, "I read a book recently. Wasn't able to grasp the content then. But now I guess, I can relate and understand more what the book wanted to say!"

"Sarika, go ahead. Relate and tell us what are your thoughts", Surbhit pleased.

Sarika explained, "The book had the term 'God in our hearts'. I couldn't comprehend it then. But now thinking about 'Joy of God' lifestyle, I can relate them.

Many of us feel the emptiness inside. Then we start negotiating with our emptiness. We address the symptom of emptiness, but never the cause of it! Typical example could be shopping. I have heard friends advising me to go for shopping when I was feeling low. Shopping does help, but temporarily, because it addresses the symptom not the cause! The one thing which makes us feel empty inside is 'Love', the lack of Love! It comes from lack of spiritual connection with the greatest source of love, God.

Biggest misery which we have today is that people feel unloved, uncared for and unwanted! The only cure for loneliness and unhappiness is Love, Love of God! We need to bring back that love in our lives. Open your heart and let God reside in it. We would feel complete.

'Believe in yourself and let God reside in your heart'.

And when we just believe that God resides in our hearts, we will see the beauty of it. We will now see whole world as our own. We will love everything we see, as we see part of God everywhere we go around, they all are part of God's soul; our brothers and sisters, joined by God's soul. We see this world as our home, where we don't just need to head off to work and come back and think only about the life of our own. We start to care about others too.

Our happiness now will come from happy and smiling faces of others. Instead of expecting more and more from life and people, now we will think more and more about 'Giving back'. Like a son trying to impress his father/mother, we would try to impress God by bringing joy in other's lives. We will be trying to impress God."

"You truly have knowledge store inside you Sarika" I applauded. "I would second that with a wonderful analogy which the holy saint had told me. He had said,

'We are to God, what woodwork is to a carpenter.'

There is a story called 'You are Special' written by Max Lucado. Do give it a read. The analogy signifies that some woodwork created by the carpenter might be beautiful, some would be ugly. But that is only in the eyes of the people who want to buy the woodwork, so they rate it. For the carpenter, all his works are beautiful! He has showered same love on all his works. It's his creation. He loves them all!

May we all understand that it's the people around us who always try to rate us and control us; our creator loves us no matter what. We must follow our heart, follow our dream, and create our own path. We should not live by the 'plan' created by others for us. We need to live our life and enjoy the 'Love' of God. God resides in our heart; we don't need people to rate ourselves. Let your creator rate you always! He would always rate you, Numero Uno!

If we have a belief in God, that God resides in our hearts; and we always do God's work which would make us the 'Joy of God', then we would be the epitome of what God would wish humans to do on this planet!"

'May, you be the Joy of God'

* * *

Chapter - III

Morning Mirror Test

We spent the evening at the Alumni meet ceremony, followed by a surplus dinner buffet. We interacted with our professors and met many colleagues. After the dinner, I looked at Sarika, then at Ayush and Surbhit. They looked back at me. I could see eagerness in their eyes. Physically we were at the ceremony but our minds were still gripped by the 'joy of god' discussion we had few hours back in the cafeteria. They wanted to know more! Their different perspectives to life was leading to a meaningful and exciting discussion. Even I wanted to learn more. Surreptitiously we slipped away from the Alumni ceremony, into my hotel room balcony.

"Dude, I couldn't even concentrate on what the dean had to say. My mind was somewhere else" confessed Ayush, with a faint smile on his face.

Sarika said, "It was not only you Ayush. Even I couldn't stop myself from pondering about the 'Joy of God' lifestyle. I couldn't even concentrate during the brief session we had for the next batch."

"I couldn't believe myself that I, Surbhit could be the source of our creator's smiles. I mean, it would be a wonderful feeling. Isn't it? Knowing in your heart that your creator smiles when he sees you!" exclaimed Surbhit, almost shouting with zeal.

"Before we discuss further, it's good that we all got some time to collect our thoughts and think more about this lifestyle" I said profoundly." By the way Ayush, I met your family-friend Shashank during the ceremony. I guess he is graduating this year. He was in the organising team and I met him backstage. After few conversations, I got to know that you are planning to leave London! Is that true?"

"Yes, brother. I always wanted to be in Indian Government Services. I have started preparing for the exam. I am planning to quit my masters in London once I crack the government services exams." informed Ayush cheerfully.

Suddenly we saw grim on his face. He continued, "But, there has been a thought which has always bothered me."

"Share with us Ayush. May be we could be of any help", said Sarika.

"When I talk to people about Indian Government Services, mostly I get back is that you cannot escape bribery. It made me think a lot. I have lot of self-respect, I would never take a bribe. But what if someone much more powerful than me offers me a bribe? I mean, I can't run away from the fact that I might be offered bribe some day. I will be offered a bribe one day or the other. My heart says 'no', but mind says that it's better not to mess with the big guy!" blurted out Ayush.

"That's very genuine concern Ayush. It's very difficult to decide what's right and what's wrong" seconded Surbhit. "Why are you smiling Amrit" questioned Sarika looking at me.

"Well, I am smiling at the timing of Ayush' concern. The holy saint had various ideas and methods, and I was about to start discussing on them.The very first method perfectly fits and probably solves Ayush' dilemma." I said.

They looked quizzically. I loved it.

* * *

I continued, "The holy saint told me that in this complicated world, one of the greatest challenges which we face in our day-to-day lives is taking up decisions or actions which are morally sound and for a greater good. We all have been advised since our childhood days to keep away from actions which are immoral or unacceptable.

But, sometimes it gets difficult to think much more than just our own personal interests. Even if we want to do good work, we often face the dilemma of deciding what's right and what's wrong.

Our world is a mix of different kinds of people. The saint emphasised a lot on the fact that,

'*Each person has good as well as evil inside. It's upon us whom we listen to!*'

If there is goodness inside you or you want to listen to the 'Good' you, then the Morning Mirror test shall be your guide. It is a conscience building method."

"Morning Mirror Test! What's that? Every morning we should test the clarity of the mirror!" joked Surbhit. This made us burst into laughter.

I continued smiling, "No brother, you don't have to test the clarity of the mirror, rather test the clarity of your character through the mirror!"

Sarika perplexed, "Please explain."

"Consider this. We often end up asking ourselves: Shall I do this or not? What will others say if I do this? What will others say if I don't do this? Will I be accepted if I do this? Or will people hate me? What will happen if my action displeases a big guy? We basically let others determine our course of actions, consciously or sub-consciously!

Sometimes taking a wrong step might bring us in limelight of our entourage, whereas taking a correct decision might make them call us names."

Surbhit added, "I agree with your point. A simple example could be the case of 'drunk-driving'. Many young people just do it to show their group of 'friends' that they can drink and still stay in control to drive! Even I did it once just to impress some folks around. Some from the group actually applaud this person by saying that he has got the stamina. In the same group, there would be a person, saying 'No' to drive, once drunk. What will he be called then? 'Coward', I guess. This peer pressure in future, might lead him to drunk-driving as well."

"We generally do succumb to this pressure of getting the acceptance by others", said Ayush.

I affirmed, "Instead of asking ourselves what others might think of us, let's ask ourselves what God will think of us! Change our perspective of life.

If we start to analyse our lives from the eyes of our creator, we would know what's acceptable and what's not! We need to un-complicate things and lead a simple life by doing things which are acceptable in God's eyes.

The saint told me to ask the same questions as above, but from God's viewpoint. *Shall I do this or not? What will God say if I do this? What will God say if I don't do this? Will I be accepted by God if I do this? will God smile at me if I do this?*

Sarika said, "But, even if we don't take a decision or a step to impress others, we might be just doing something without giving it a second thought."

"Absolutely. It's sub-conscious at work. Many a times we 'react' to a situation automatically, rather sub-consciously.

Just wait a moment more before 'reacting' and think twice before taking a step. Then 'respond'.

Our each and every miniscule decision could have some impact on someone else's life. Let's take the example of drunk-driving or breaking up a traffic signal. At least the driver should understand that he is not only putting his own life in danger but more than that; he is risking life of someone else too, maybe the pillion or a person crossing the road. Remember that we are born to make this planet Earth more lovely and beautiful place to live in. Let's make sure our actions strive to do so, always!" I said.

"The holy man had said that,

'*How can we be joy of God if our day-to-day actions are not helping our mankind?*'

When we take a decision just to impress someone or without a prior thought, while it might hurt someone else! Let's first see how we can always try and take the correct path in life, a path which our God approves of. Let only God help you in determining the correct path in life."

Confucius[1], the great Chinese thinker and philosopher had said -

> *"If there is righteousness in the heart, there will be beauty in the character.*
>
> *If there is beauty in the character, there will be harmony in the home.*
>
> *If there is harmony in the home, there will be order in the nations.*
>
> *When there is order in the nations, there will peace in the world."*

Sarika shared her thoughts, "I think when we don't care about people's opinion of us or our actions, our sufferings would alleviate. It would be such a pain just to live the life set by others; trying to appease others, always denying one's true self.

For a change, we should live for ourselves. Let God decide what is right and what's wrong; let God be our judge and guidance in life. Let us stop appeasing others; a thousand people have a thousand mouths and thousand different wishes. We would never be able to fulfill everyone's wishes, they would never end. Let's make our life much simpler. *Let's just care about what God, our creator, thinks about us! Let's just do that.*"

"Yes, Sarika. Let's just do that! And when you do that Ayush, you will get a reply from your heart whenever you face a dilemma. Listen to it!" I said.

"I will keep that in mind. But how do we perform this 'Morning mirror test'?" said Ayush with a gentle smile.

Surbhit added, "But same moral value does not works in every situation. What is correct in one situation can be very wrong in another. So, we can't have a fixed moral values for all!"

"Indeed Surbhit. Indeed. Morals, ethics and duties can vary from situation to situation, from region to region, from country to country. We should not generalise a moral code for everyone. Each heart is different and each heart's connection with God is different! That is why I believe that Morning Mirror Test can be very useful. For every situation all you have to do is not look into any book for a correct behaviour or guidance, rather look within, and look in your heart to find the truth!

This is a simple test which we can follow each morning. The holy saint called it 'Morning Mirror Test', a soul purifying test. This would help each and every one of us in deciding what's right and what's wrong through God's viewpoint."

* * *

I continued explaining the Morning Mirror Test, "The holy saint said that to be most effective, this test should be performed early morning as soon as you wake up."

Every morning as you wake up, go to a mirror and look, look deep in your eyes. In the mirror you directly see your eyes. Eyes are said to be connected to heart. You can see a person's heart in his/her eyes. And who resides in our heart? God! So through our eyes, we can directly connect with our creator every morning! Look deep inside your eyes into your heart, God. *At this moment there are only two persons who could see you and can judge you: yourself and God* !

Now you can be true to yourself. You don't have to act as you do in front of other people. It's just you and God. God knows all. Your heart knows all about you and your actions. There is no scope of lie here. Just stand in front of the mirror, and ask your heart:

"*Were all my decisions or actions taken yesterday true to my heart?*"

The holy saint quoted, *"You can lie to everyone, but not your eyes in the mirror. They know the truth!"*

Sarika asked, "Wouldn't our mind try to justify our actions?"

I replied, "Of course, it will. Mind will try to justify your action, give various excuses. But, who are you lying to in front of a mirror! You need to be true to yourself. You can lie to anyone and everyone, but not yourself. Your heart knows the answer when you ask yourself this question. Don't try to justify your actions.

If your heart says that you have done something wrong, then learn to accept it. There is no bravery lost in accepting one's mistakes. No one is born perfect or is perfect, at least we can strive to be better than what we were yesterday! Let this 'Morning Mirror Test' be the guidance by God in our lives."

Surbhit added, "I guess, even after doing this test many won't want to change themselves and keep ignoring their heart."

"That may be very true for some. That's why I said earlier, if there is goodness inside you or you want to listen to the 'Good' you, then the Morning Mirror test shall be your guide.

Let me quote Swami Vivekanand[2] on this,

'Why should a Man be Moral? Because this strengthens his will.'

We must remember that by performing this test we would feel more connected to God and are striving to be the joy of god. Decision still resides with you, whether you want this love of God or not."

Ayush inquired, "Is it difficult to follow?"

I replied smiling, "It is difficult to follow what God wants, what your heart wants. But you say it's difficult because you are thinking what people would feel, when they would know that you take decisions by performing this method! What will they say if they come to know that you follow this test? For a moment, if we leave the 'opinions of others' aspect out then this daily test is not at all difficult.

In fact, it would guide us in a positive way and we would know what to do when in doubt in every situation! We don't need a book. All we need to do is consult our heart! And this will keep us calm and composed, as we know deep down that God approves of our actions. See, our job to impress has become so simple now. We just need to impress two as compared to hundreds of people. Just two: Yourself & God! This test is that simple. The holy saint has been following this method for years now!"

Sarika impressed her thoughts, "I think it's like a test before God each morning, each day! The final test of life is not any school or college exam, neither acceptance by any person; the final exam is acceptance by God when we would be before God, and via this test we could do that each and every day! I guess, this daily mirror test will be a preparation for our final test before God."

Surbhit said, "Let's say that after performing this test, I get a directive from my heart. What should I do then?"

"If you aren't able to see your eyes in the mirror, you know what you have to do! Your heart is not approving of something which you did yesterday. Depending upon the situation, you can either correct your mistake today or pledge to never do the thing again. You have a new day today, to correct all your mistakes; so that when you look again in your heart tomorrow morning, you could see your eyes! Let God judge us and our actions, and guide us."

Surbhit interrupted, "But this test only checks our decisions/ actions already performed! How can it guide us beforehand?"

"Excellent question Surbhit. Look at this way. It can also help in determining our course of action beforehand. As we have known about medicine that 'prevention is better than cure', same fundamentals apply here. Prevention of a wrong step is much better than amending its effects later on.

Before taking up any decision, we should just close our eyes and imagine doing a 'Morning Mirror Test'. Then, ask yourself:

"Will my soul, my heart and God permit me to do this?"

"Will God be happy with this decision of mine?"

"Will my action make a difference in someone else's life, in a good way?"

"If I do this, will I be able to look into my eyes tomorrow morning?"

Mahatma Gandhi[3] had once said-

"Recall the face of the poorest and weakest man you have seen, and ask yourself if this step you contemplate is going to be any use to him."

Steve Jobs[4] had once said about reflecting self through mirror –

"I have looked in the mirror every morning and asked myself: "If today were the last day of my life, would I want to do what I am about to do today?" And whenever the answer has been "No" for too many days in a row, I know I need to change something."

I concluded, "There always will be a good and bad inner self talking simultaneously to you. It's upon you to decide whom you want to listen to. This mirror test helps you to notice that faint voice of the good inner self, and do what's the right thing to do. Listen to it!"

* * *

Sarika added, "I think performing this test on a daily basis, would be a revelation in our lives!"

I seconded, "Upon applying this test, we would feel a new beginning to our lives. This test would add a new dimension to our lives."

Ayush said, "But in the beginning we might get 'No' for most of our questions to self!"

"That's very true. When I started performing this test daily, I used to get answers which showed me that I was not on correct path earlier. I wasn't happy with many of my decisions and actions. The start of this test might not be an easy ride. The answer 'Yes' to these questions are very close to ideal situations, which might seem difficult in the beginning. In the start, we might mostly get 'No' as our answer. Please don't stop if your answers are 'No'. This test is a preventive-corrective measure and guidance for our life."

Sarika added, "Earlier we might be taking steps without a thought about it; hence our answers might be more inclined towards 'No'. But, it's not impossible to reach 'Yes'. After we start taking this test daily, our sub-conscious mind would every time start contemplating our actions and decisions beforehand. We can always correct our paths. The biggest problem is that people cannot comprehend when they are wrong. This test would tell us in a matter of seconds!

We can take a corrective course over a period of time, by daily practicing this test. We would slowly move towards 'Yes'. Our answers would slowly turn towards 'Yes', which would imply that God approves of our actions or decisions. We would be inching towards being the 'Joy of God'."

"Very true Sarika. If the answer is 'No', then we must check our steps and take the right decision. It might sometimes be a difficult one, but in the end our heart would be at peace! We would feel proud of our self for doing the right thing.

With God watching over us, we would know deep down that God is happy with our decision and loves us even more for the decision. Remember, that this path to 'Yes' might be a difficult one and our will, strength and patience might be tested. Just do the right thing thinking it as God's work. And, God would smile at you!"

Surbhit had another doubt. "So to get back to a correct path in life, how long do I need to perform this test?"

I replied, "Surbhit, this is a lifestyle. This never has an end. It should and must go on to become your daily chore; a test before God, daily. This way, every morning as soon as you wake up the first thing you would do is connect to God! And your actions in the next hours or the day would also think of the outcomes and you would do what is good for this world and the whole humankind. Slowly, this test would turn into an integral part of your life, correcting you, preventing you and guiding you towards being a good human being. We would always be true to ourselves, and this would bring inner peace to our heart.

Personally, this has brought lots of positivity in my life and my lifestyle. This test has helped me to get out my dilemma, and strive towards being a better person. Doing good work would always make God fill with joy, and you would be the reason for this Joy!"

'May, you be the Joy of God'.

* * *

Chapter - IV

Gratitude: A Way of Life!

We were still sitting in the balcony lingering over our thoughts, when the doorbell rang. I had ordered coffee for us. The room service man poured us coffee and reminded us that the kitchen was opened till three in the morning in case we wished to order something else later. We all thanked him for his prompt service. He obliged with a big smile and left.

As we took the first sip of our coffee, Surbhit exclaimed, "Dude, did you notice the big smile on his face!"

Sarika said confused, "Yeah, I wonder what was going in his mind!"

I said, "I guess, I have got a fair idea about that smile." They all looked at my face with curiosity. I continued,

"It's called Gratitude. The power of Gratitude. Let me explain this from the service man's point of view. He is working here late night, probably awake whole night to serve the guests better, which is his job. But not many appreciate his effort I guess. When we all thanked him, he must have loved being appreciated! Simple. Our 'thank you' created a positive vibe. This is the next method which the holy saint told me about. Gratitude."

Ayush said happily, "So you mean to say that our gratitude brought smiles on his face! Amazing. Isn't it?"

Surbhit said, "And how exactly does Gratitude helps us be the joy of God?" I was expecting this question next.

* * *

"Well, before discussing about gratitude let's talk about 'fear'. We all are in a constant fear of something or the other. We might be in fear of getting hurt, of losing something we own or bringing bad luck in our lives. We are afraid of our stars bringing bad luck and suffering to us.

Out of fear of wrath of God, many try to please God by performing numerous practices. Have you ever thought whether these practices, done out of fear, really make God happy? What does God really expect from us, humans? *Only love and compassion for each other.* Why are we in constant fear of God?"

Ayush said thoughtfully, "You have struck a chord my friend. I guess many of us do perform these practices because deep down we fear the outcome if we don't perform them! Practices are part of our culture, but they shouldn't be performed due to fear."

"Exactly Ayush" Sarika seconded. I continued, "The holy saint used to say,

Would God be happy if we just perform practices due to the fear of bringing bad luck if we don't perform them?

Would God be happy if we remember God only to ask for more and more? Would God be happy if we just seek God in difficult times?

There should be only one reason for us to remember or seek God, only to show our love and gratitude to God for our blessings in life. Gratitude!"

Surbhit queried, "But what does make us fear God and perform practices just to appease him?"

"The holy saint used to say that there is always two ways to think about the future; one is to think that something bad could happen and the other is that something good could happen. By default we humans have a tendency to think about what bad could happen. Whereas thinking about a good outcome is a real challenge as our mind often wanders to think again about what bad could happen!

So we generally tend to think that something bad might occur if we don't perform certain practices, that God might be unpleased if we don't do some rituals. This makes us fear God more, than love God!

Tell me something, will this negative thought process and fear bring Joy to God?"

Sarika shared her views, "We basically need to train our minds to be optimistic and always remember that it's not necessary that bad luck would come to us in future, and there is an equal probability that we can have good luck too!

If we have 'belief' in ourselves and are aware that God resides in our heart, then why fear! When we have equal probability of bad and good in future, why tire self with bad thoughts. Think of something good and beautiful."

"So true. The holy saint told me, *'Believe in yourself'*. Why fear God? We all are God's sons and daughters. God resides in our heart. Why can't we be God-loving? It's same as loving our parents. Show God some love. Instead of fear, fill your thoughts with love. When the fear goes away from heart, we would see what gifts God has given us. We are special to God! *It's time you thank God from the bottom of your heart.*"

* * *

Ayush continued on, "You mean to say that many are god-fearing instead of God-loving."

"Yes Ayush, sadly many are! Gratitude is a simple way to love God! Gratitude is simple way to be the 'Joy of God'. We should be thanking God for all that we already have. We should not search for God just for the sake of asking for more and more. We should go in search of God to thank and be grateful for our blessings and gifts!

The holy saint often told that *if we visit a temple, mosque, church or any other religious place, we must remember to thank God then and there for ten different things before we ask for one more blessing in life.*

We must learn to be grateful first and stop being greedy for more and more."

Sarika said, "What about those who turn towards God only in time of crisis situations?"

"We should not remember God only when bad times come, hoping that God would come to our rescue. We should remember God always, in good times as well as bad times.

In good times, we must thank God for the happiness and success that we have. Also we must thank people who helped and supported us to achieve this good day! In bad times, we must remember that God resides in our heart. This would give us the courage and strength to wade off hard times. Once we succeed, we must thank God again for being the strength and courage! We all should love God and thank God for all the things which we have got."

Surbhit confessed, "Seems little awkward that we need to thank God! At this moment, I am not able to think of things to thank God! How should we thank God?"

I explained, "Let me give you some examples. We can always start being grateful with saying to our heart "thank you for continuously pumping and keeping me alive!"

Surbhit interrupted, "But heart beats for all, why should we be thankful for that?"

Sarika was quick to answer, "Well, that's the very reason we need to be thankful for. As you see, heart beats for all people, who are alive! For those, heart doesn't beats, are no more. So thank God for keeping you alive this day!"

Ayush said, "How can one kick-start this gratitude thinking?"

"It is rather very simple. Let's list down what normally would be our daily routine, and see how we can be 'thankful' for the circumstances. This is just an example, you can always find out more instances in your life to be 'thankful' for. Let me take you through a simple daily routine and find instances which should be a reason you to thank God.

- As soon as you wake you, thank God for the bed underneath you, the blanket covering you and the home for keeping you warm, safe and sound.
- As you get up, thank God that you are alive to live another day.
- Thank God for your legs and arms, these help you to do your daily chores.
- When you see the beautiful sky above, thank God for your eyes!
- When you hold your toothbrush, thank God for your teeth.
- When you shower, thank God for clean water and clothes.

- When you go out for work - thank God for giving you a vehicle or for the public transport system in your city. Thank your government too, for public transport services, the traffic lights and the policemen.
- Thank God for keeping you employed! If you don't feel thankful for just being employed or working, then look for a newspaper and find out the unemployed percentage. At least the reality would make you accept your blessing of being employed. We take a lot of things for granted.
- When you eat your lunch - thank God for the food and keeping you healthy.
- Thank the food vendor for providing you a healthy and hygienic food. Thank the washer for cleaning the utensils in which you ate.
- When you go back home, thank God for giving you the family to go back to!
- When you go to shop and you get a discount. Thank god for making you richer by saving your hard-earned money."

I continued, "You can find numerous books and articles available about gratitude. They all talk about the power gratitude has and how it can change lives! And, the above mentioned list can go on and on. I would request you take some time, think and make your own list of blessings now."

Surbhit said, "Like 'now' now?"

"Yes brother. Go ahead. The holy saint had said in a poetic way,

'Whoever you are,
Whatever you be,

Wherever you are,

You can always find a reason

For being thankful.

Be grateful, tirelessly!'

He told me that we all must strive to make 'Gratitude' a way of life. A simple thank you can bring smile on someone's face. Remember the face of the service man? Let's make this world a happier place to live in", I concluded.

* * *

I handed each of them a piece of paper and pen. Meanwhile I ordered some more coffee and some snacks for us. We all four sat there in complete silence pondering and scribbling over our piece of paper.

After ten minutes or so, Sarika expressed, "If we can just focus on our life for a moment, we can always think of so many blessings to thank God. I am myself so amazed about the gratitude list I just made. These blessings were always in front of my eyes, yet I hardly ever noticed them!"

I said, "Make gratitude your lifestyle. Thank God tirelessly. When we start to thank for one blessing, our mind opens up to various other possibilities and then we realise that we have many, many more blessings to be thankful for!

This process will slowly make us believe that god truly loves us and has given us so many gifts in life. Slowly our fear of God would transform into love for God. Instead of only thinking about what negative that can come, we would start to thank God always and every time for what positive we already have in our life!"

* * *

Ayush said, "I think I have a story which depicts the power of gratitude."

"Great Ayush. Please share the story. It might help me understand much better", said Surbhit.

Ayush continued, "One morning while going to work, I was walking past a temple, where I saw few beggars outside. There I saw a man giving ten rupees to two beggars sitting near the corner of the temple. In their native languages, first beggar said, "what would happen in just ten rupees? Living is too costly nowadays". The second one said, "thank you for your generosity". Next day as usual I was again on my way to work, when I saw the man again. The man gave some fruits to all the beggars around.

I noticed this change and asked the man about this. He replied that the second beggar was thankful, so he gave more! He was happy to serve them."

I said, "These were the exact words which the saint had told me,

'The attitude of someone in gratitude is inspiring.'

We all like if someone acknowledges our help or service to them, whatever the impact or size of help be. And that acknowledgement inspires us to do more and more!

Our creator is all-giving. We shall notice more and more reasons to be grateful for if we just acknowledge and thank God for the blessings that we already have now! This is the way to see life's beauty too. Unless we are thankful for what we already have, we won't be able to see the beauty in our life and love our life. Once we thank God and acknowledge blessings that we have, however small it may be, we will see the beauty of life. We will see our heart peaceful and content. We will see God's hand in support of ours. This would inspire us to do better work and achieve more success and happiness in life."

* * *

Sarika said, "Even I have a story which could help us understand the impact of being in gratitude and the loss when not being in gratitude!"

"Wow Sarika. Please share the story" exclaimed Surbhit.

Sarika continued, "At my workplace, there was a wonderful group of new campus recruits. They used to laugh always and be happy, they were full of life. When they used to go to cafeteria for breakfast, lunch or snacks, their group were the most happy and bubbly in the whole cafeteria! It was happiness around them.

After one year of service, it was time for their annual appraisals and ratings. This rating was a yearly process. Each year they would get a rating. When they got their ratings, some of them got rating 'two' and some got rating 'three'. Rating two being better than three. If you see economically, the salary difference between rating two and three was around Ten Thousand rupees in a year. But in that group, few people were upset with their bad rating, and this started creating an air of jealousy and tension in the group. Over a period of days, they laughed less, enjoyed less and in a few months' time, the group broke. Sadly!"

I pitched in, "As I stated earlier that '*the attitude of someone in gratitude is inspiring*', similarly the negative impact of being ungrateful can also cause lots of problems and miseries."

Sarika continued her story, "Now, what we see in the above story is the difference between the two ratings. Have we forgotten to consider something? What about the difference between previous salary and the new salary (say, with the lower rating three)? Well, it was one lakh rupees. Isn't that a sufficient reason to be happy and grateful? On one side we have a salary hike of one lakh rupees and on the other side we are less than ten thousands.

Few in that group used to say that their rating three is not justified compared to the others who got two! So here are two sides of a coin, two perspectives. One, by comparing self to others and bringing misery. Second, comparing self to your prior self and being grateful!"

Ayush said this time, "I think, *Life is a choice.* Even finding things to be grateful for is a choice and an art. We should all strive to master this art of finding a God's gift in any and every situation we face in life."

Sarika continued further, "Here is another story to complement prior one. During the same time, there was a friend of mine who had been unemployed since one year after his graduation. Seeing the peer pressure and social pressure that we have nowadays, I was very worried about him. I was aware of his unhappiness. But, he always had a smile on his face. I loved his courage and patience. After almost a year of struggle, he finally got a job couple of months back."

Sarika then said, "See the two situations above. Second situation person, had no job at all. First person at least had a job plus a salary hike of one lakh. Still, first person chose to overlook what they got! They chose to be ungrateful. Their ungratefulness caused a lot of rifts in their group."

I put in my views on the story, "This attitude is not one-time thing. We could be ungrateful for many things in life and overlook them. This would make us sadder. Gratitude should be a way of life. It can help us to transform our thoughts and bring positivity, happiness and love in our life.

Just imagine if everyone thanks God for smallest of things in their lives, how beautiful world this would become. How happy and joyful God would be to see his sons and daughters content and happy and grateful! We take lots of small things for granted. Let's start being thankful for the small things as well!"

Surbhit asked, "So how do we pitch it in our daily lives?"

I replied, "I guess, every morning as you wake up, just give few minutes to God. Start with the 'Morning Mirror Test'. Then try to thank God for at least five to ten different things, daily. You can thank about your job, education, health, relationships, money or anything. Just find a reason to be grateful for. You will be amazed how blessed you have been!"

* * *

Ayush asked, "What we learned just now was about showing gratitude towards God for our blessings. What about people who help us in our day-to-day chores? Like the room service man."

I said, "Excellent point Ayush. We all saw the smile which our gratitude caused on the face of the room service man. The holy saint iterated this many times,

'Gratitude should be an attitude! It should be a way of life'.

The holy saint said that gratitude is something which has now been lost in the history. Life has moved much ahead of the initial, great civilisations. What our ancestors understood since they walked on this earth, the knowledge of 'Gratitude', has been lost now. Our forefathers used to thank the Sun for giving us light. They thanked the Sky for rains, which helped them in harvesting crops. They thanked mother earth for giving them a shelter to live on. In our times, we just take these for granted and seldom thank god. We should always be conscious to the gifts we have got. We should always be thankful."

Sarika said, "Yeah. I think somewhere we humans got so busy in materialistic development that we took our blessings for granted!"

I continued on, "The holy saint said that we should not only show our gratitude to God, but also to other people as well. Even a small kindness shown to us or any service done for us, should be rewarded with gratitude from our side. It is not only about showing gratitude to our creator. We should be conscious to services done for us by other people as well. We should also be in gratitude to people who help us in any way."

"A person might be doing his job by giving you a service like your office food vendor or a plumber or carpenter. The person delivering us the product we purchased online is just doing his job making sure that we receive our product timely. The pizza delivery boy might have driven very rash and risked his life just to make sure your pizza reaches on time! Just say 'thank you' the next time you get a service with a smile. It will create a positive vibe.", I cited.

* * *

Surbhit was eager to know more. He asked, "What else the holy saint had to say about gratitude?"

I thought for a moment when it occurred to me. "Oh, I forgot to mention something very simple yet amazing words he told me.

The holy saint said, *'A simple 'thank you' is the greatest prayer.'*

Your gratitude would bring smile on the person's face. A single thank you or an act of gratitude grows exponentially."

Surbhit said, "Hey, I have actually witnessed the growth of gratitude which you are talking about. I understand it better now. Let me share the incident with you all.

I was in a coffee shop near my office campus. There was a man sitting few rows in front of me. He had ordered coffee. Now, it's the job of the waitress to get the order. I had often seen the waitress and she always seemed to be dejected. When she brought the coffee, the man said 'thank you' with a pleasant smile. Immediately I could see the waitress smile. I think it made her feel appreciated, and who doesn't loves to be appreciated for his work!

It was a heck of day and the coffee shop was filled with customers. She was very busy and had hundreds of orders to attend to. Yet, she had a smile on her face and happily greeted each one of them. She even thanked many for giving her the opportunity to serve them at the coffee shop. I guess, it was that first 'thank you' which motivated her to work better and with all her heart. She became charming and cordial to her customers. Even I was among those whom she thanked. I had never seen her that chirpy ever.

After leaving the coffee shop, I went to a burger stall nearby. I felt obliged. I thanked the waiter at burger stall for his service. I guess, even he too had a wonderful day and served his customers with full heart and compassion. I think, this is the growth of gratitude which spreads so rapidly and created smiles around!"

I applauded, "Wow Surbhit. That was a simple yet amazing story. It shows how a single act of gratitude can travel miles and spread smiles around!"

Ayush was next. "Let me share an incident which happened with me in a local bus.

I had to go to a coaching centre to prepare for the government services exam. I was travelling in a local city bus and the bus conductor came to collect the ticket. He asked for change amount very rudely. Even though I had change, I got reluctant to give him seeing the rudely behaviour. He started abusing me. His behaviour set off my mood a lot. When I reached the coaching centre, I was still feeling upset and angry at people around, the traffic, my studies anything which came in my way.

After a few hours, a guy in the same coaching centre came to me and said, "Hey, I was in the bus too! I saw what happened. Let it go man" I felt anger at this person now. Before I could respond, he said that there was a reason why the conductor was rude. Even the conductor had a minor altercation with another passenger just before I boarded the bus. The earlier passenger didn't have any change. When conductor asked for change, the passenger instead of being politely saying that he hasn't any, started cursing and abusing conductor for not keeping the change!

So what we can see here is that gestures propagate from one person to another. If one polite gesture can link up to bring more smiles, then that would be your bit to make this world a happy place. Had the passenger politely said that he is sorry for not keeping any change and thanked conductor upon receiving the ticket, the conductor would had felt good about his job and in turn would had been good and polite to other passengers as well."

I was happy to see that they were able to relate the teachings with their personal lives. I said, "*Just do your bit.* Just say 'thank you'. The cycle would proceed on itself. Never think what would happen with just one 'thank you', as many people don't say it! Just think that your thank you could grow from one person to everyone, slowly but surely."

As usual Sarika had her excellent views. "Many times we don't appreciate and acknowledge what we already have. Time passes and if in future we lose those gifts, blessings or people, then we realise their importance in our lives.

So, we must start today and thank God and everyone around us. Show God and people that you appreciate and acknowledge their help and presence in your life. Else in future, you might feel sad when you realise that you have lost something, a gift or a blessing or a person, and you never got a chance to say 'thank you'.

Even if you feel sad at this point, at that very moment start thanking God for those beautiful memories, blessings and gifts in your life. The memories which were giving you grieves would now make you smile."

I concluded, "That is the power of Gratitude. It can transform lives. It can cause a much vibrant and happier world that we live in. It is amazing how one word could change our world in such a great way, but that's the power and magic of this word. That's Gratitude. Make it your way of life. Try and look for reasons to be grateful for. Do your bit. It will create more and more happiness and love, and God would be smiling and proud of you."

The holy saint had a wonderful poem on gratitude,

May you thank for every service.
May you thank for every help.
May you thank for every gift.
May you thank, thank & thank more!

May you create a thousand smiles,
With your gratitude!
'May, you be the Joy of God'

* * *

Chapter - V

Giving Back

It was getting a little cold in the balcony. We all moved into the room and continued with our discussion along with our coffee and snacks.

I said smiling, "Well, the Holy saint mentioned another method which accentuates us in being the 'Joy of God'."

Sarika said, "Amrit, the first two methods of 'Morning mirror test' and 'Gratitude' talk so much about the way we lead our lives. And they don't seem to require much effort either. They fit so well in our hectic lives!"

Ayush replied, "Amrit had told us initially itself that these ideas and methods is a way of life, a lifestyle. Also that these could be easily incorporated in our daily lives".

Sarika continued, "I know. And I second that. I am excited to know what the next method has in store for us."

I said thinking, "I guess, the involvement in the next method could vary from person to person as well. But, in the simplest way it is still a good fit in our daily lives.

The saint talked about 'Love-Hate Circle'. Imagine a circle of 'hate'. You hate someone or perform actions out of hatred on someone. The person would receive your hate or the effects of your hatred would impact his life. He would go ahead and perform a hate action on the third person. Similarly, the third person would go ahead and do the same to the fourth person. And so on and so forth, until it reaches back to you! This is the circle of hate. What you sow is what you reap! You let out 'hate' in the world and you get back hate.

In the same way works the love circle. You spread love and smiles around. It will traverse from first person to the second person and then to the third, and later on unto you. This love-hate circle is what we are going to discuss now. What we are 'giving back' to the world, love or hate!"

* * *

I started, "Our every action or failure to take any action, decision or shying away from taking any decision impacts people around us and our society too. 'Giving back' signifies giving back something 'good' to society, and humankind."

Ayush said mockingly, "Give back! We always tend to ask for more and more from people, society and God. We always tend to blame government, people or God for our misfortunes or poor luck. That's how many of us give back!"

I continued, "So from now on, let's stop asking for more, acknowledge what we already have and start 'Giving back'."

Surbhit said, "But many may not have much money to indulge into 'Giving Back' activities. Some are busy in their lives and don't have time for all this."

I said with a smile, "The holy saint told that Giving back is not only about serving someone in need, financially. He said that we can give back in various levels to our humankind. Simplest level being, the monetary help, where you contribute to alleviate someone else's miserable condition, fund a child's education or vaccination, provide food or clothes and so on. The next level could be to teach someone, imparting knowledge. That's why teachers should be highly respected and valued. Remember an old saying, 'Give a man a fish, and you feed him for a day. Teach a man to fish, and you feed him for a lifetime.' The next level of service could be to enlighten a human mind spiritually. Not everyone could do this, but we all could lead our day-to-day lives in such a way that we could inspire others to lead their lives in a good way.

Think about great people like Mahatma Gandhi, Mother Teresa who inspired the whole world from their way of leading life. It can be spending some time with the underprivileged time to time, morally support them and making them feel loved. It can be feeding a beggar you see on the street. It can be helping a blind man cross the street. It can be teaching your kids good moral and social values, so that coming generations could have a good and healthy society to live in. It can be anything which could serve others, our society in any way. Just think and find a way to give back.

You don't need to carve out specific hours for 'giving back' activities. Many of them can be incorporated in our day to day lives."

Surbhit questioned. "How much should we give back?"

Sarika was quick to answer, "There should be no bar to decide whether our impact is big or miniscule. What matters is that we impact society in a good way! If every person vows to even make a small impact, imagine the combined impact of all. Our world would be a happy place to live in, for all. There would be love, generosity, care and joy everywhere."

Ayush said sadly, "There are some who 'give back' their bitterness."

I said slowly, "Some people do give back, but in a negative way. They spread violence and miseries around them. That's why it is equally important that we have people who give back goodness to the world.

We must let go off any bitterness inside us. If we let this bitterness grow then it would eat us and we would go on to give back too many miseries to the society. We won't be bringing Joy to God by spreading violence or miseries around us. God wouldn't smile at that!

If something bad happens then please don't give back the 'bad' to society, as revenge. Wait for your opportunity to be good again. Wait for the times to be good again. Everyone has a bad phase in life. A bad phase doesn't mean that we can cause miseries to others around us in return. Just imagine if everyone starts to give back in a negative way then where will world end up to?"

Sarika shared, "I think that some people give back in a negative way because they feel apathy or antipathy for the people around them. Apathy or antipathy, both occurs due to lack of love. They don't feel connected to this world and people. They do not love what they are seeing before their eyes. There is lack of love of God in their lives. They are not connected to God. Only love of God can inspire us to lead a meaningful life. Let's always strive to feel that love of God in our lives, and live to be the 'Joy of God'."

* * *

Surbhit asked, "What is the simplest way to 'give back' good?"

Trying to frame my reply properly, I said, "Charity is one of the most obvious and easiest ways which can help us to

'Give Back' good to society, financially. Charity is done to help and raise money for poor and needy."

Surbhit said, "But why charity? Why should we do this? Why should I give away my hard-earned money? I already pay tax."

Sarika said thoughtfully, "The answer lies in the fact that we all are united by the God's soul. It is like helping out a brother or sister in need. If we don't help our poor and needy brothers and sisters, then who will! We pay tax to our country. Charity is to humankind, and beyond geographical boundaries!"

Ayush was next. "So, how much charity is enough?"

I said, "Whatever we could give would be a God's work. People donate as per their convenience, some donate big amounts, and some donate small amounts. Doing charity is important. But, to give a rough figure, I would say around 3-5 per cent of income should be donated to charity. If anyone can give more, that is always welcome."

Ayush asked, "So can you tell us how one could start doing charity?"

I said with a smile, "Of course, if you live in India, you can check out the 'GiveIndia.org' site to navigate and donate to various NGOs and charitable organisation in our country. Employees in big firms also have the option of opting for schemes like 'employee giving programme'. There are international agencies like 'World Food Programme' (wfp.org) who work all over the globe. Just do your bit."

Sarika said, "Just imagine if every earning person donates 3-5 per cent of their salary, then our nation, this world would be place which God had always wanted us to be: helping out and taking care of each other, making this world more beautiful, lovely and amazing place to live in!"

* * *

Ayush was intrigued. "Does charity really create an impact?"

Sarika replied, "Let me share a story. Once I was registering at an NGO in Bangalore. The NGO worked for welfare and education of poor girls. I asked the person the yearly cost for the education of a child. He replied that including school fees, school clothes and books the yearly cost comes around seven thousands rupees only. That's like Rs 600 per month only!"

Surbhit exclaimed, "Wow, we generally spend more than that if we just make a window shopping trip to a mall on a weekend!"

Sarika continued, "Exactly. Can't we just afford to give this minimal amount monthly? Can't we curb our personal expenditures a little bit, and carve out this amount monthly? We can! It might not create a big dent in our expenses, but it might be a life-savior for someone in need!"

I said happily, "Let me share another story. A journalist questioned *Mother Teresa* the impact she could have on our society, alone. There is still too much suffering and poverty in this world despite her social efforts.

Mother Teresa[5] had famously said:

'We know only too well that what we are doing is nothing more than a drop in the ocean. But if the drop were not there, the ocean would be missing something.'

What we would be giving back to the society might have a small impact, like a drop in the ocean. But that ocean is incomplete without our drop. If each one does his drop, the ocean will be complete!

Let this message guide us and always motivate us towards social work and making the difference. We must remind ourselves that the world needs us. Go out and create an impact. That ocean is incomplete without your drop!"

* * *

Ayush said, "I know a couple of folks who do charity but they don't like to publicise it in front of everyone! Why is that?"

Sarika said, "That is very true. Some people do charity but they don't bring this side of their life out in the world! They say that they don't do this for their own publicity."

I pitched in, "First of all, we all must appreciate and congratulate them for indulging into charitable activities. But it is a fact that charity is still not done by many people. Many think that someone else would do it, why should I give away my hard-earned money.

Imagine if there is a group of four friends and one of them donates to charity. If he talks about his charitable work in the group and few more get inspired and join the charity work, then he has helped to enroll more people for the good cause. We need more helping hands, many more. We need 'word-of-mouth' publicity for charity, so that more people could do charity for good causes.

Personally, I have always been telling people around me about the various charitable organisations I am donating to. Many friends have come back saying that even they wished to do something for the society but didn't know how! That's where the 'word-to-mouth' publicity for charity helped them."

Sarika said, "This is a God's work we all are doing in doing and publicising charity. We need many helping hands for a greater good. Let's try and bring all hands which we could."

Surbhit seemed to be thinking something. He said, "But how do I know that my money would be spent for the right purpose? What If the charitable trust is corrupt? I want to donate, but want to make sure that each paisa is spent on a needy or underprivileged?"

I had an answer to that. "I have a friend Nitin and I loved his way of performing charity. First of all he connected with those charitable organisations which were near to his living place, so that you could visit them whenever he wanted to. Then he chose the charity which was close to his heart – education for underprivileged children. He was able to see the impact his money was creating in this world. Some weekends he himself went to these children, taught and played with them!"

Sarika said, "We still might not be able to know where each paisa is going, but connecting with a charitable organisation makes us see how our money is being helpful to someone in need."

I continued on, "Let me share another story. It's a story of an Orphanage in the outskirts of Bangalore called 'Balya Children Home'. As a CSR (Corporate Social Responsibility) initiative, once I visited this orphanage where they provided home and shelter to orphans. They also opened a special school for the kids. The owner told me how he was moved to tears and started this orphanage.

Couple of years back, one fine evening, he was walking to his home with his wife, when they heard a faint cry of a baby. They found a week-old baby lying on the pavement and crying in the cold night of Bangalore! They took the baby to their home and thus started their journey towards providing love and compassion to orphans.

When I saw the smiles on the faces on young kids, I knew these smiles have been a gift to these children from the owner and more so ever, these smiles motivate and inspire him to help the young kids tirelessly!"

Ayush said, "I think visiting places and connecting with charitable organisations whose cause is close to your heart makes much more sense. There are organisations working for various causes like child education, girl protection, environment, cancer patients, orphanage, and blind schools etcetera. We must try to connect with a cause which moves our heart. Helping for a cause which you believe in, would help you also to grow as a person and give you a sense of belonging. The cause close to our heart would inspire us to do more and more. It would become like a never ending appetite of 'giving back' on and on."

"Wonderful explanation Ayush" Surbhit said happily.

* * *

Ayush asked, "I have read in some books the term 'power of giving'. I guess, they talk about giving back."

I confirmed, "Very true. The holy saint told me that true happiness can only be found in service of others.

Present day economics has made happiness equivalent to the gadgets we could afford, the services we can get, the shopping we could do; all materialistic. Is it Happiness? Maybe! But evanescent happiness! It will fade away. Once it fades away, you will again have to buy a new gadget or go for shopping."

Sarika buzzed up with excitement. "Let me tell you a short incident which happened to a close friend of mine. It was his birthday. He was out buying groccries for his Birthday party that day. When he came out of the mall, he saw a school going girl holding a donation box for cancer patients. Thousands of people were crossing in front of her. They all had shopped for thousands of rupees! No one gave a second glance to that girl. My friend was also among these people.

But, he felt bad and went over and dropped a hundred rupees in her donation drop-box. She smiled! And he smiled!

He went on and gave a great house-party that night. Then he told me later that the happiness of throwing a great party was nothing when compared to the happiness he felt after donating hundred rupees in that box! He couldn't forget the smile he had caused on the young girl's face. He was smiling constantly because for the first time he felt what it feels like to bring smile on the face of someone else! His heart was smiling! He was Happy. Not an evanescent happy, but an eternal happy!

He always tells me that it has been many years now but he still smiles whenever he imagines the smile he caused on the face of that child. It's an eternal happiness for him. This one smile had inspired him to put more efforts to his charitable works. That's the power and joy of giving."

"Wow, I wish I could be the reason of someone's smile" thought Surbhit.

I concluded, "So, let's stop thinking so much about ourselves and start doing social work and spread the word about it. We need more people to help out our poor and needy brother and sisters.

The world needs us, God needs us. Let's not be quiet in the work of God. Let's shout out loud and let the whole world know. Even if one out of ten joins social work, you can smile! Let's start our chain reaction of charity. Let us change this world. You and me, let us spread more love and happiness in the world. We all need some!"

* * *

Ayush said, "I also read about the 'joy of sharing' sometime back."

Sarika remembered something. "Guys, do you remember the nursery rhyme 'baa baa black sheep'?"

I was puzzled. Ayush asked, "Why are changing the discussion? What does this nursery rhyme has to do with the joy of sharing?"

Sarika said in utter excitement, "Everything! Let me play it now on YouTube for you all. Notice the lyrics."

After the rhyme got over Ayush said, "Wow, we have been taught since our childhood the importance of sharing. This nursery rhyme has an important message in it. It's a rhyme which teaches us the joy of sharing, giving, caring, helping and loving."

I said, "Let me quote Mahatma Gandhi[6] on this:

"To find yourself, lose yourself in the service of others."

We all are busy in our lives, have plans for the day. Sharing our 'time' seems like a big task. Sharing our precious 'time' with people in need is a service to mankind and God. It might not be practical to share our 'time' on a daily basis. We can always plan to give a few hours on weekends. Sharing our time and love, can bring out lots of beautiful smiles in this world. If we do not take care of each other then who will!"

Surbhit suddenly lightened up with a smile. "Guys. Even I have an incident to share which shows that impact which sharing some 'time' can bring!"

Surbhit continued, "A group of my colleagues, who actively take part in community services, decided to organise some fun events for patients in the last-stage of cancer at a hospital care facility in Mumbai. The patients had a wonderful time, laughed and smiled a lot. For a moment, they were living again! For a moment, everyone was cheerful and lively!

The very next day, a member of the group got a phone call from the hospital. A man whose uncle was admitted there, wanted to talk to them. The man told him that his uncle expired just a few hours after my colleagues went back from the hospital. But the man thanked my colleague!"

Ayush asked the obvious. "Thanked! Why?"

Surbhit said, "The man said that his uncle died in peace, and with all the physical pain that he was bearing, he passed away with a smile on his face! The man thanked him and his group members for making his uncle have a good eleventh hour of his life.

The 'time' my colleagues spent with the patients made them feel more loved. Everyone craves for love. Love brought smile on the face of a dying man."

Sarika said little emotionally, "I think we all should spread more love around. We always have special plans for a long weekend, or a festival or holidays. We must enjoy these moments to the fullest, but as we learned tonight that we should also carve out our time and money for 'giving back' so that we could make this world a much happier and beautiful place. When you would see the smiles, you would know that those smiles are there because of you. You are causing joy and happiness. You would be the 'Joy of God' for spreading love and smiles around."

She concluded, "This is the power of sharing. It can only create more joy and bring smiles in this world. Wouldn't God be happy if we 'Give back' good to world? Wouldn't God be happy if we help and support our brothers and sisters? Wouldn't he smile back at us then? Wouldn't we be the 'Joy of God'?"

'May, you be the Joy of God'

* * *

Chapter - VI

Bitterness, Anger and Frustration

It was almost midnight, but we all had our flights back late afternoon the next day. I had time to share further. I continued on, "Let's talk about giving back 'bad'!"

Sarika exclaimed, "Giving back bad! But why? How does that help us create smiles and happiness around?"

I said, "We all know it doesn't. But let's talk about it for a moment. I would rather ask a question. Please think about someone whom you think has given back 'bad' in this world."

Surbhit said, "Okay. Done."

I continued, "I want you all to describe in one word which could have caused the person to give back 'bad'!"

Surbhit said, "He must be feeling bitter about what happened with him." Ayush thought and said, "He had lots of anger in him." Sarika prompted, "He was frustrated."

* * *

I noted down the three words 'Bitterness, Anger and Frustration' on paper and began,

"While it's perfectly human to feel various emotions, we should know how to control ourselves. Bitterness is one such feeling, which should be kicked out of our heads as soon as it enters it.

But there are a few time, where we think that the outcome wasn't something which we deserved. We see some people less deserving, but they get more than us, much more than what they actually deserved. This could also lead to feeling bitter about life as a whole. There could be many more reasons which could make us bitter, and when we feel bitter we generally go on to say that 'life is not fair', or 'it's a bad day today'. Remember the rating two and three story we discussed sometime back."

Sarika seemed puzzled. "I still don't get how is this connected to 'Joy of God'?"

I said, "It's not directly related. In terms of mathematics, I can say that being 'Joy of God' is inversely proportional to being 'Bitter, angry or frustrated'!

Let's first understand what happens due to our bitterness. How our own bitterness is impacting people around us or the society in whole? Due to bitterness, a person generally tends to think: 'something bad happened to me, I will also give back 'bad'. God gave the other person more when I was more deserving. I will try to find out a way to take my vengeance.'

This is just one instance of bitterness and it's like 'Giving Back' in a negative way. If something bad happens to a person, and he would start to take revenge or get even by giving back the 'bad' to someone else in his anger! When we give back to society in a negative way, be sure that God isn't happy. The more we feel bitter, the more we go away from being the 'Joy of God'.

Let's look at the wrath and crimes against women in our society. Most of these crimes occur due the bitterness prevailing among men. Some men say that these crimes happen because women entice them by wearing revealing clothes. Some say that women roam late with their boyfriends. Some say that their boyfriends have permission to touch her then what crime they did by touching her! These men are bitter that she agrees to be with some other man, but not them. Most of the 'Acid attacks' are done on women by men who have been rejected by her.

I have a request to all men to stop seeing a girl as an object and try to respect her as a human. Why do we go on and show our frustrations on a woman? There is bitterness prevailing in some men which leads to the crimes against women. See the impact of bitterness on our society. Is this going to bring joy to god? No. We must learn to curb our bitterness and never give back to society, people and world in a negative way. Only then we would be able to create a world full of harmony, peace and love. Then God would smile at us."

Sarika said, "Believe it or not, but the more we feel bitter the more we would start seeing things to be bitter about. We could feel bitter about not having a decent job, a car, a house or about anything we come across. If we let bitterness grow, it would feed on us! It's just our perception of things and life. All we need is another angle to look at our life."

* * *

Surbhit asked the intelligent question. "How can we stop or say, control bitterness?"

I said, "The holy saint said that '*It's all in the mind*'. We need to change the perspective, the outlook of our lives. It's not about whether life is fair or not. We should enjoy our lives no matter what."

Ayush said enthusiastically. "Hey, I remember a story on life being fare or not. I had heard long back during summer vacations from my grandmother when I used to visit her in my village when I was a kid. It exactly talks about how to control the feeling that life is fair or not! Let's learn from it. It's called 'an old man and snake'."

He continued, "Once there was an old man who had a poultry farm and a shed for his animals near his house. He had been well fed, well respected and lived happily.

One evening, while returning back he heard a faint voice beneath his legs. He removed a stone below to see, and found an old snake. The snake had no strength to move away and asked the man to save him and take him out of the hole and feed him some milk. The old man was weary of snakes, but seeing the plight of snake, he thought against it and helped the snake.

As soon as the snake was out, it circled around the man's neck and said smiling "I am going to feed on you now". The man got very scared and said, "But, I saved your life. You can't feed on me. It's not fair."

Snake laughed at him, "Who says that life is fair. It isn't."

The man tries to convince the snake again, "at least leave me. I just now saved your life". The snake replies "Okay. Find me one animal which says that life is fair. I give you chance to ask three animals. If anyone says that life is fair, I would let you live." The man was hopeful now. He thought that he had many animals in his farm. The man went ahead with the snake around his neck to his farm.

He first met a cow and asked 'Is life fair?' The cow looked at him slowly and said "well, I am being fed grass everyday but in turn you take away my milk. I am being looked after well now. What about when I grow older? When I am of no use to man? You will then send me to the slaughterhouse. Life isn't fair". The man couldn't disagree with the cow and moved ahead. The snake had a wicked smile.

The man moved on and found a dog. He asked the dog same question. The dog replied, "Well, I am not a stray dog. The family feeds me well; I play with their kids in their lawn. But, what about when I grow old? I have heard that humans leave their old dogs on roads to die! Is this the worth of my years of obedience and service? Life is not fair at all." The man became very anxious now. Snake hissed to farmer "one more and then I feed on you."

The farmer found a bunny and asked him 'Is life fair?' The bunny looked at him and replied "I am not grown enough to understand whether life is fair or not. But once I asked my mother and she said that it does not matters, whether life is fair or not, whether you are happy or sad, whether you have what you want or not. All you need to do is get up and dance, enjoy life!" and with that the bunny started dancing.

Seeing him, the man along with snake, cow and dog started to dance. The bunny found a moment when snake was busy dancing his tails off, and flee away with the man."

Sarika said happily, "What an insight about life! Dance, sing, laugh and enjoy your life. It would take away most of our miseries. There is no point is keeping our bitterness inside us. We must let it out so that it doesn't affect any other person."

I said, "The holy saint often said that if we could understand the outcome of our bitterness, anger or frustration only then we will know why we must curb and control it. It hurts our good judgment too. When bitterness comes to reside in our feelings, anything and everything starts making us angry. We are then under control of vengeance. All we could think of now would be of giving back 'bad'. Any decision at this point of time would never result to good judgment. We might end up spreading more hatred in this world! That's not what God would want. That is not going to make god happy. That won't make you the 'Joy of God'."

* * *

Ayush said, "I'm lucky that I am aware of an incident which clearly shows how a man drank his bitterness and never let it out."

Sarika exclaimed, "Really! Go on and share with us. We all need some inspiration now and then."

Ayush continued, "I was driving in my car to my office. I was speeding past a signal to refrain from getting stuck in the signal before it turns red. In this haste, I did not notice a bike on my left. I noticed him very late and applied brake, but in that split second my car hit the bike.

Luckily, nothing happened to the car, the bike or the biker. But the biker fell off his bike. He got up gently and said...wait! Let me ask each one of us. What would we do had we been that biker?"

Surbhit said, "I might have started a verbal spat with him and may be more."

Ayush had a mischievous smile now. He said, "Now think that you were driving the car. You had just hit the biker. What are your thoughts now?"

Surbhit said shyly, "In my case, I might try to flee away from the signal as soon as possible."

Ayush said, "I just wanted to know how we look at the same thing from different perspectives. But, let's continue with what actually happened!

The biker got up and looked at me. I apologised. I understood it was all due to my fault and apologised again. I was speeding because of the worry of being stuck in traffic and being late to office. I apologised! The Biker came closer to me. I was mentally prepared to get a good amount of beating from public that day. Something strange happened then. He said 'It's okay. As long as you understand it's your mistake, it's okay!'

Sarika said, "Really?"

Ayush confirmed, "Yes. Even I was surprised by his demeanor. He simply drank all his anger. Amazing being I must say. Now, let's discuss two aspects here. I guess, my apologetic nature helped a biker, who might be feeling angry. Then thinking from the biker's perspective. He got something unexpected and something which could make him bitter and angry. Just imagine a morning like that, where something bad happens the first thing you get out of your house! But what he did, he overcame his bitterness! He just let it go! Had the biker been bitter about it, he would have created a ruckus there and that would have made me bitter or angry too. And this cycle of bitterness would have continued."

I said, "We all must thank to you both gentlemen that you spread love and smiles around. I'm sure many watching this scene at the signal would have learned how to control bitterness and anger."

I continued, "This reminds me of what the Holy saint had said once,

'It's not easy to get hit and then stand up again, smiling at life.'

Life will definitely hit us somewhere and sometime. But, now you already know that! So, get up and smile at it. That would be your greatest victory."

* * *

Sarika said, "I guess, like bitterness even anger and frustration should be kept in check."

I affirmed, "Cent per cent true. Being angry and frustrated can never spread love and harmony around. The negative energy of anger and frustration reaches people around us. We must focus on spreading only love, harmony and smiles around. Spread the positive energy around us. It's our choice what we wish to spread in this world. When we feel positive, we spread that positive energy around. Smile, love and spread harmony and peace.

When we feel negative, there is lots of negative energy inside us. We must check ourselves from letting this negative out of us to people around us. Anger and frustration might come to us any moment of the day. We should learn how to curb this negative energy from spreading out."

Surbhit intrigued, "You said sometime back that these feelings are natural. They come to everyone. We have to check them. How do we exactly check anger or frustration?"

I replied, "We should learn to channelise our negative energy in some other way which is not harmful to anyone, and prevent it from letting it out and spreading to people around us.

A twenty minute jogging or an hour of walk always helps me to channelise my anger or frustration. It helps me to channelise my negative energy which is not harmful to anyone; plus jogging/walking keeps me healthy.

The next time you feel anger or frustration, remind yourself that if you let it be inside, it would grow and grow more, and hamper you and everyone around you. You won't be able to spread love and harmony then. Try to push this negative energy out of you, but away from all. Try to jog, exercise or work out when you feel anger or frustration. Spread only love and harmony around. Only then you would be the Joy of God."

'May, you be the Joy of God'

* * *

Chapter - VII

'Me' Time

The discussion got so interesting that we all forgot to check the time. It was almost one in the night. We decided to put a brake now and get back to our respective rooms. It also gave us time to think about the ideas which were discussed today. I agreed to continue with more ideas the next day. We agreed to meet for breakfast at eight in the morning.

I had a very peaceful sleep. The message of 'Joy of God' had been inside me since days and months. I felt so relieved to share this philosophy, this lifestyle with my dearest friends. With a smile on my face I slept like a baby that night.

* * *

The next day, we met for breakfast. We all sat around a table with a cup of coffee and smiles on face. I could see a glint of sparkle in their eyes. They were all beaming with the new found knowledge to help them connect with their creator.

For some time no one spoke. All the heads were busy, thinking. But I had to break the silence because I wanted to discuss further! "You know what phase we all are in now? Where you take lots of personal time to look within."

They had puzzled looks on their faces. I continued, "It's called 'ME' time. A time for self.

Swami Vivekanand[7] had said:

'Talk to yourself atleast once in a Day. Otherwise you may miss a meeting with an EXCELLENT person in this World!'

And this is what the holy saint advised me to do a lot."

Ayush was perplexed. But before he could ask his obvious question. I said with a smile, "In our day to day lives, we generally forget to connect with our inner self. To connect with God, it's important that we are able to connect with our inner selves first!

And how do we connect to ourselves? Talk to our heart. Listen to the faint voice of the heart. If we could talk to ourselves, it would be great help to channelise the distress and bitterness too. It's necessary that we take out a 'ME' time from our busy schedule and talk to self. It helps us to reflect on our actions. It helps us to talk to our inner self."

Surbhit did ask the question. "How does talking to self, makes us the 'Joy of God'?"

I continued, "Let's first see what 'ME' time can do to us and how it can impact our lives. After we understand the importance the 'ME' time and talking to self, then we will deduce how it can make us be the joy of God. Let's explore."

* * *

I said, "The holy saint that we just live whole day in a mechanical way following a set routine, without connecting with self or God. We forget to make time for self. In all this, we forget to hear the faint voice of our heart. We forget to have some time for self, 'ME' time. We forget to 'talk to self'. We forget to look within and know self. We sometimes neglect our dreams.

From today, let's give ourselves some time: 'ME' Time! Let's try to listen to what our heart wants to say. Let's try to talk with ourselves regularly. Let's try to reason our actions with ourselves; it will help us to improve our actions, decisions and our path in life.

Like the 'Morning Mirror Test', when we take out 'ME' time for ourselves we are in contact with ourselves, our soul and God! Connecting with our heart brings its smile on our face. Our inner and outer self is one now. So let's start by connecting with self through 'ME' Time. We would then be connected to self and answerable to self! Like Morning Mirror Test, we would weigh the impact of our decisions when we talk to self. We would start to impress ourselves first!"

Surbhit said, "I generally take some lone time when I feel sad."

I said thoughtfully, "We are the reason of our own happiness. List down things which makes you really feel good. We can call it a '*happylist*'. Personally, top positions on my 'happy' list are music and ice-creams. For an immediate effect, I generally tend to have ice-creams and listen to 'Sonu Nigam' songs to find my calmness and to feel good."

Sarika said cheekily, "I love to eat when I feel low!"

"Next time when you feel low, just do the things mentioned in your 'happy' list. When we start to feel better, we must remind ourselves that God is always there to back us. We should not worry. Remind self that no person or circumstance could make us cry or disheartened. We are too strong for that. Tell yourself that. If life can be hard to me, then I can show that I am much harder to break! Tell yourself that" I said.

Ayush asked, "What about 'ME' time when I am happy. What do I need to tell myself then?"

I said, "First of all, we must be humble in triumphs or success. We should never let success make us forget the people and circumstances which helped us reach here. The holy saint said that,

> *'If we can row through a rough river, then our strength and courage is appreciable. But we should not forget the 'oars' which helped us to achieve this feat!'*

Similarly in life, of course it's our hard work and skills which can bring us success, but there would be people and circumstances that would have helped us in some way or the other in our journey towards success. We should not forget to be grateful to them. We must thank God and people because of whom we are happy today. Remember, this is a way to connect to God. Whenever something good happens, have a 'ME' time and remind self to be humble and grateful.

Don't get negligent in the flashlights of success. Nor get too engrossed in the want of more and more success, money or power. Remind yourself that it's equally important to enjoy and live the moment God has given to us."

Sarika had been little quiet the whole morning now. It was her turn to put in her thoughts. She said, "I was still thinking about 'ME' time when I feel sad or dejected. I think it's equally necessary to pacify our heart when our life is hit by a storm. 'ME' Time is very useful at this moment.

Talk to your heart. Our heart trembles a lot. We should strive to pacify our hearts during rough times. Tell yourself that God is within us, that God resides in our heart, that God always has a plan, that whatever happens, happens for good. Tell yourself that the turbulent times would give way to placid, bright and sunny one. God has plans, always. Just 'believe' in God's plan. Take out some time to remind self that."

I added, "More than anything, we should never put blame of our failure or bad luck on people or circumstances. Try and introspect. Find where you went wrong. Learn how could you correct and improve self. Life is a never ending learning process. If we don't make mistakes then how are we supposed to learn!

It's time like these which are the real test of our character! Whenever you face difficult times, talk to self during 'ME' time: "So, I have got this problem. Let's see how I can mitigate it." Never get pegged down by hard circumstances.

I remember that the holy saint told,

'Diamonds are created under heavy pressure! Let this time be the pressure which could make you shine like a 'Kohinoor'!'

Sarika said, "Sometimes, it takes time that your hard work pays off. You might not see immediate results of your hard work. Tell yourself that the work done is laying down the foundation for future. The seeds sowed will reap fruits in future. Tell yourself that."

I concluded, "If something is disturbing you, then always think that it was God's hand that your life took this course. So be happy. It will become your own good. God loves you. We all are God's children. As a child trusts his/her parents; we should have same trust in God's plans. Always remember this advice in adverse situations.

In adverse situations it is important to keep calm and not feel dejected and down. If you believe in your heart that there is God's hand in whatever happens, you would know that it's a God's plan. You would know that things will work out.

Like the holy saint said, '*Keep calm and trust the Plan!*'

* * *

Surbhit asked, "Can the 'ME' time help me when I don't feel inspired or motivated?

I replied with a smile, "We must remind ourselves what motivated us in first place! We nowadays take up activities on impulses and short-lived inspirations."

Ayush said, "The most common motivation we can see in people is when it comes to gym, exercising or jogging regularly. Seeing the fitness of famous actors/sportsmen, people generally get inspired to start exercising in most cases. Generally, this effort lasts for a week or month. People lose their initial motivation in most of the activities they incorporate in their lives."

Surbhit was intrigued, "That's very practical nowadays that we lose inspiration in short span of time. What shall be done if we start to lose our motivation?"

I said thinking, "De-motivation can only cause problems. Feelings which were discussed earlier, like bitterness, anger, frustration, loneliness will surely find a place in our lives if we stay de-motivated to live our lives. Hence, being de-motivated would never lead us to being the 'Joy of God'. That's where 'ME' time can be of great help to us.

We are the only one who could motivate ourselves the best. We might be inspired by some people or circumstances, but the ground work for success and happy life has to be done by self only. There can be many inspirational people, stories or circumstances, but the actual motivation to do something good can only be done by self.

Only our own voice can motivate our heart to achieve great success and triumphs in life. We can read many inspirational quotes and feel good reading them, but in the end only we can make self to actually follow those great thoughts in our lives.

Only we can do what we got to do! Talk to self. Practice 'ME' time daily. Inspire self, daily."

Surbhit had a query, "What happens when we are already motivated to do something? How is 'ME' time helpful then?"

That was tricky. "When we are down and de-motivated then 'ME' time could come into picture to calm us down and motivate. It's equally important to practice 'ME' time when we are cruising towards our goal. Being constantly motivated in the long run is important.

We could lose focus or the inspiration to keep moving forward in the long journey. 'ME' time can make us live a day or a moment at a time, motivate us to conquer short-time goals, which would later lead us to our ultimate long-term goal. It would help us to be on track."

* * *

I was trying to think of something which the holy saint had told me once. It was eluding me. Suddenly it came back and I said, "You know, the holy saint said to ask self what really makes you happy during 'ME' time.

The holy saint had continued to ask me, '*Imagine if the whole life has to be spent in helping and living for others. Wouldn't that make God happy?*'

In our fast-moving daily lives, we forget to connect with our creator. It's not about worshipping, idolizing, praying. It's about connecting with God, simple! 'ME' time can help us to focus on our lives, our strengths, our blessings and God. It's about seeing the gifts that God has given to us, seeing the power that God has, and seeing the power that God has given to each and every one to shape their own destiny!"

Ayush said astonished, "Seeing the power that God has given to each one of us to shape our own destiny!"

I said with a smile, 'Yes. We all have the power. Look within yourself. You will see what a masterpiece God has created. You, my friend, is a 'carpenter's' masterpiece!"

Surbhit added, "We are Humans, What power do we possess?"

I said, "We have the power to shape our own future, our own destiny. We have the power because we are all sons and daughters of God. We have God's in us. God resides in our heart. A body with God inside in heart can shape his life in whichever way he wants.

'ME' time would help us reconnect with ourselves and make us believe and feel what beauty we humans are! All we need is 'Belief'."

I concluded, "Let me recite a poem which I wrote recently".

A belief,
That I have the power
That I am magnificent
That God is in my heart
A belief, that I need not be afraid
A belief, that I am Son of God
That I am God's creation
A belief, in me!
A belief in self
Is all I need.
That I am the center of
Love and generosity
That people are delighted
By my presence
That I spread smiles & happiness!
That I am the 'Joy of God'.

I read this poem to myself during 'ME' time daily. I just takes me half a minute. I read this whenever I wish like.

'ME' time would help us to weigh the impact of our decisions. It should remind us to be humble and grateful in success and triumphs. During failures it would help us to be courageous, patient and always learning from our mistakes.

'ME' time shall remind us to help and support our brothers and sisters. When we practice 'ME' time, we are actually connected to our soul, which is connected to God. So, we actually talk to the God residing in our hearts.

In simpler terms, it's a chat with God! 'ME' time can be done anytime and anywhere. It would be just you and God, talking.

'May, you be the Joy of God'

* * *

Chapter - VIII

God is One!

We took a small break to pack our luggage and decided to meet at my room in an hour. Within an hour, all came to my room and we sat again in my balcony.

Sarika made a green tea for herself. She was reading the morning newspaper and some news made her face tensed. Sipping the tea she said, "I was thinking whether hatred towards other religions is going to make God happy?"

I smiled thinking the timing of this question to kick start the discussion. I said, "Our world has many religions, each with various cultures and traditions. Each of the Religion has a different deity to pray to and worship. History has witnessed many instances of intolerance among the religions. The holy saint asked me once,

'Will fighting among ourselves make us the Joy of God?'

He said that any harm done to another being can never bring glory to God. A fight to display the superiority of one religion over other can never bring Joy to God. Our soul has no religion. It just knows one thing that it is a part of God. Religion is by birth but our soul is eternal. In this birth you are a Hindu, the next you could be a Christian or a Muslim or a Buddhist. Religion is not for the soul. Soul only knows God. A fight in the name of Religion can never bring Joy to God."

"I have a story which could help our understanding better on this" said Ayush. He continued, "A mother of two grown-up men invited them for dinner. First one was a renowned school teacher and the other was a successful financial consultant. Whenever the brothers used to meet, they always tried to demean each other.

During the dinner at their mother's place, they had an altercation over a petty question 'whom does mother loves more?' This question went from a simple conversation and tease in the beginning to fist-fights and brawl by the end. The scene was a horror for the mother to witness.

Let's wait a moment. Another person present there asked the mother, 'Who do you love more?' She replied with a tear in her eyes, "I love both of them alike! Both are different but they are my children, they have my blood. They are my sons!"

I think we all are different from each other. But, we are made like that, different."

"So true. Some would be hard-working, some would be smart, and some would have a beautiful heart etc. Some people shine like a diamond, some help others shine! God has created each one of us different, capable enough to make our own decisions. Try to appreciate the difference in people.

When it comes to different religions, let's show some tolerance towards people with religion other than ours. In the end, they all are our brothers and sisters. We all are different and diverse. Among all this diversity, there is a link which unites us all, all the religions: God, One God!"

* * *

I continued, "I remember that the holy saint always said,

'Religions are like Rivers!'"

Surbhit questioned perplexed, "Religion and rivers! What kind of analogy is that?"

I replied happily, "Let's look at the relation between rivers and sea. All rivers flow with a single aim, to reach the sea. Our religions are like the rivers, and God is the sea. Like all the rivers flow with the single aim of uniting with the sea, same goes for all the religions in this world."

Sarika exclaimed, "That means we all are like different rivers, but with a single aim: to unite with our sea, God. God is one!"

"Yes. Let's learn something more from rivers. Firstly, we know that many rivers bifurcate into rivulets, but still all aim to unite with the sea. Their paths diverge in their quest, flowing through different terrains and lands, but only with one aim: to unite with the sea. Likewise, history has seen birth of many different religions and many different religious practices, but we all still thrive to unite with God. Religions may flow in different paths, tread different people, but eventually they all move forward and strive towards achieving the same aim, uniting with sea, God."

Ayush said, "So basically God is one, but there can be many ways to unite with God."

Sarika appended, "Yup. And no path is greater or mightier than the other. They are just different! The other path is just a choice different than yours! Let us learn to accept the difference and strive to flow in harmony."

I continued on, "Secondly, there are many streams which come together to form a river and then flow towards their goal, the sea. When they join, there is turbulence and clashes in the river, but eventually they unite and flow towards their common aim.

We have seen many communal and religious clashes in this world. We need to eventually maintain harmony and peace, and always remember that every religion and tradition aim is to achieve a common goal, uniting with our God. We must accept and respect other religions and strive to flow together, hand-in-hand in our path. Streams unite to form a greater force, so that they could reach their aim else they might not be able to go the distance! Similarly, we all are sons and daughters of God. We may follow different path to meet our creator. Why not do it hand-in-hand, with peace and harmony!"

Surbhit exclaimed, "Wow. Never thought that a river could teach us so much about religion!"

"There's more!" I confirmed. "Let's recall how rivers are formed. A river can be perennial or seasonal. A perennial river has water sources as glaciers, whereas a seasonal river is dependent on the rains. How are the glaciers and rains formed? The source of water in form of rains or glaciers is precipitation, common source for different types of rivers. God has given same source to rivers, but when flowing on earth it takes different paths and forms! And in the end they unite with the source.

Similarly, God doesn't differentiate among us. Our source of life is same: God. When on earth, like rivers we have different paths, religions. When we have the same source, how are religions internally different from each other? All religions have same source and same core teachings and the same ultimate goal! They may follow different paths, different religious practices. Still all are same, internally. In the end, as rivers all religions too have single aim to spiritually connect with God, to unite with their source of life."

Sarika said, "In a holistic view, we all have a common source, God. We are born on earth and follow different cultures, religions and practices. But in the end we all aim to unite again with the God."

* * *

Ayush asked, "If uniting with God is the ultimate aim then why are so many fearing God!"

I said, "A God-Fearing person is religious and a God-Loving person is spiritual. Religious and spiritual are two different faces of a same coin."

Ayush perplexed, "Please elaborate on that."

I continued, "A God-fearing person is a simple being, who is caught up in the web of chains that religion has built around us. He follows the religious cultures/practices as taught by priests, without questioning or a thought! He acts because he is afraid of the wrath of Gods, if he doesn't acts as holy priests say! It's not wrong to be a God-fearing person. This is good, as this keeps people away from sins and crimes. But, this is the only merit of fearing God. There is no other reason that you should fear God!

For a society to grow and prosper we need to have both God-fearing and God-loving persons. A God-loving person can be God-fearing too, but a God-fearing person can never feel being God-loving. But that does not convey that a God-fearing can never become a God-loving. Eventually, if he could understand and see the love, care and protection of God instead of just seeing wrath, he would start loving God instead of fearing! When the world tries to make us God-fearing, this 'joy of god' lifestyle strives to make us a God-loving person."

Surbhit asked, "Does a God-loving person performs the religious practices too?"

A tricky question I must say. "A God-loving person may not perform religious practices and norms because it's a religious ritual. His actions are just to please God. Love for people and God motivates his actions. They are spiritual beings. They wish to be the 'Joy of God'. They are God-fearing also, as they will never do things which would make God sad and unhappy! It's their fear that they would cause unhappiness to God, if they do any sin or an immoral act. God-loving persons feel the love of God upon them, they feel God's protection, they have faith and they have 'belief'!"

* * *

Ayush inquired, "Can a God-fearing slowly turn into a God-loving person?"

I said happily, "Of course, anyone can. First of all, it's okay to be a God-fearing person because that's the first thing that society teaches us about God. That's the first step anyone takes. But the next step is to love God and unite in the end! It's a step-by-step process.

All we need to know that anyone can step on the path that leads to being 'God-loving'. That can happen if we start feeling the blessings that God has given to us. We will then understand the love and care God has for us. There are few steps which we can do daily to feel God's love and support in your life:

- Start your day with thanking god for making you live another day!
- Think about the things which helped you the day before. Things which made you feel blessed like job, security, health, city transport, love, relationships, friends, food. Anything which you could think of !

  Thank God for these blessings. Make 'Gratitude' your way of life.

- You can always perform the 'Morning Mirror Test' and 'ME' time as explained earlier."

Surbhit asked, "So how does these steps help?"

"These simple steps would make us feel every morning that God has some part to play in our lives. We would start to feel connected with God. We would start to see our blessings and gifts in life. We would feel that we are alive this day because God wants us to. We would 'believe' in self and God's plan. Slowly we would start loving God! Slowly we would have many reasons to love God rather than fear him! And, remember that God always loves us!"

Sarika said, "But there are some people who magnify the God-fearing aspects!"

I said, "Yes, there are. A God-Fearing person needs to understand what some priests tend to do. Some priests ask us to do things by magnifying the effects of 'Not-doing' so. They make us fear God. They know our weakness; they know that we are God-fearing people. They make us fear more! Sadly, religion has become more like a business venture these days.

But that does not mean that the intention of religion is wrong. Religion helps us bind with God, but why fear God? Why fear your own creator? We all are his son/daughter, we are God's children. We must fear only of doing a sin. Don't fear the effects of not performing a religious ritual or practice. Those were made by humans only, not by God. God just wants us to be good and spread love around."

I continued on, "The holy saint had a wonderful thing to say,

> *'Fear God if you sin. You shouldn't fear god if you don't follow some religious practice.'"*

Sarika shared her views, "A parent loves, cares and protects its child, and punishes if children do something wrong or immoral. God is our creator. We shall feel God's love, care and blessing in our life. Then we won't fear God, and just love God.

Bring joy to God by loving him from your heart, and not by worshipping inspired by fear."

I said, "The holy saint recited a poem to depict this,

May you remember God
Every moment,
May you work to impress God,
May you live to Love,
May you sing to spread harmony,
May you dance to spread cheer
May you Love God,
May you fear your sins
'May, you be the Joy of God'

* * *

Surbhit seemed little confused, "Isn't being religious and spiritual the same thing. What's the difference?"

I replied, "Religion and Spirituality should go hand-in-hand. They should complement each other, not compete. Both have the same aim, to help us connect with our inner self and God. Religion should guide us towards spiritualism. Similarly, being spiritual should guide us towards being more devoted to God and being religious.

Religion should show us ways to connect with God. It should act an intermediate between us and God. There is a difference between showing devotion to God by being religious and by following some religious practices or customs. As we discussed earlier, just following practices won't take you anywhere near God, unless you are truly devoted to God from the depth of your heart. Be religiously in love and devotion to God."

Ayush asked, "We have so many religions on our planet, like Hinduism, Islam, Christianity, Buddhism, Sikhism, Judaism and many more. All are different religions having origins in different times of history and in different parts of the world. They are like various rivers flowing towards a common aim, the sea. These religions differ a lot in their practices and customs, but the underlining message is same in all!"

I shared, "Very true. I recently read the ten teachings[8] shared by all Religions:

- One God
- God is Everywhere
- The existence of soul
- God is inside of us
- Spiritual knowledge is accessible to everyone
- God's name is 'I AM'
- Compassion and respect for everyone
- Morals: Don't Kill, lie, steal, covet
- All of humanity is united
- Peace and nonviolence

All the Holy Scriptures: Hinduism's Shrimad Bhagvat Gita or Islam's The Holy Quran or Christianity's The Holy Bible; whichever Holy text you would read, all have a common saying. All emphasise on the teachings mentioned above. To understand this more, try and read the holy texts from other religions too. Reading other religion's holy texts would help us to understand people and their religion. It would help us to forget the differences and remind us that each has the same goal; to unite with the sea, God!"

Sarika said, "I think these ten universal teachings could guide us well. The next time while following a practice or custom or making any decision, do ask yourself: "Am I following the 10 universal religious teachings?" It shall help and guide us."

* * *

Surbhit asked, "Why have we been given different cultures and religions? If we all are from same source: God, then why were we made to follow different paths?"

"Surbhit, we aren't different internally. We all have God's soul in our hearts, and we are all God's children. We are just following different paths on earth, nothing more. Different cultures, traditions and practices. We have different paths to follow because we have different roles to play in God's master plan. We all are playing a part in God's plan. People in different religions and cultures, are all playing a part in God's plan."

Surbhit thought for a moment and inquired, "When everyone is playing a part in the God's plan, then what the benefit of showing intolerance and hatred is?"

Sarika replied, "Many people try to misinterpret the Holy texts and incite or provoke to spread religious intolerance and violence. These are people with devil inside them. These people with devil inside have no religion, as they don't flow like a river to unite with a common sea! As we are talking about God in our hearts, there are also some with devil inside. We must understand that we need to hear the 'god' in self rather than 'devil'."

"We all are like a team, where each player is having a different role to play in. A team can't win if players start fighting and encouraging hatred amongst each other. We are having different paths because that is God's plan. Let's show tolerance and love towards each other and live in harmony. Do you think that instead of flowing together with love, harmony, tolerance and compassion, we fight among ourselves then God would be happy? Would you then be the Joy of God?" I concluded.

'May, you be the Joy of God'

* * *

Chapter - IX

God has Plans, Always!

We had another round of coffee and continued with our discussion. We had to depart in an hour. Ayush wished, "Life would so easy if we could understand why our life takes a specific course? If we could understand why something happens in our lives and some not? If someone could tell us what's the reason of my existence?"

Sarika exclaimed, "It would be wonderful if we could get answers to these questions. The answers to these questions would help us to lead a motivated and inspired living. It would make us feel as if we belong in this world, that we have a purpose in this life."

I said, "Let's try to understand the fact that whatever happens is as per God's plan. The knowledge and belief in this fact should guide us to a happy living. It would help us to understand the cycle of time, which is like a wave having ups and downs. It shall teach us that happy and sad times are part and parcel of life. It will help us to understand that crying or laughing is our choice, and only ours! The more reasons we find to be happy, God would give us much more reasons to be happy. It's the power of thoughts. Like thoughts attract like circumstances."

Surbhit queried, "I guess, knowing this idea is also going to make me 'Joy of God'?"

I said thoughtfully, "Believing that God always has a plan, would show that we have a belief and trust in God. We would be aware that there is a God's plan. During good times we wouldn't forget God and be grateful. During bad times, we would never leave hope or loose trust and belief in God. The holy saint asked me once,

'Wouldn't God be happy and feel loved, when God sees his sons and daughters trusting and believing in him?'

We must also consider the effect of believing and trusting God's plans on us."

Ayush asked quizically, "How is that going to affect us?"

I said, "The feeling that whatever happens is as per God's plan, that whatever happens is for greater good, would also make us feel loved and protected by God. We would be laughing and smiling in all situations as we would know that whatever happened, it happened for a reason.

We have always had many blessings from God, but now we would be more open and aware of them. Our lives would be happy in the love of God, like a child in the embrace of his mother. A mother loves, cares and nurses her child; so does God!"

* * *

Surbhit said, "Let's discuss on the cycle of time. You have been wading off the subject since yesterday. Tell us now!"

I laughed in my reply, "I had been wading off so that I could discuss it now, along with understanding 'God's Plan'. Let's discuss the cycle of time.

Time is linear in our world, but what repeats is the nature of it. For a person time can be either in a good phase or a bad phase. How we behave during these phases reveals our character and belief in God. The cycle of time is a test of character.

We all are born on this planet for a reason, for a purpose. We have a role to play in God's plan! Always believe that. Everything happens, whether good or bad, is as per God's plan. We always play a part in this plan. If this world is a stage, then we all are puppets in the hands of God. Some play a bigger role, some play a smaller one. But all are directed by God! We all are part of God's plan."

Sarika said, "I believe that time is never constant, it's either good or bad!"

"Exactly. It keeps changing, so does our lives and fortunes. When we have a good time, it is because the God's plan wants us to be in! Enjoy these moments but also prepare for the time to change.

When this time changes and we face a bad time, remember that this phase is also going to change. Good times would return again in our life. This bad time is as per God's plan, as the good time was! Never get disheartened by a bad time or if anything bad happens in our life. It is all part of God's plan and we all are playing a part in this."

Ayush pitched in, "We all should be aware of the cycle of time always. We should be aware that time repeats in the cycle of good phase and bad phase. Do you guys remember the story of 'Ant and the Grasshopper'?"

Seeing confused look on our faces, he continued on, "The grasshopper just enjoys the good times, stays flamboyant and never worries that good time would change. Grasshopper never thinks that summer would give its way to winter! But, the ant does. Ant knows that times would change, and it is all part of the plan. So instead of cursing and blaming God and circumstances, for bringing bad days in her life, and she anticipates them and prepares for it beforehand. Grasshopper on the other hand, would enjoy the good times. But as soon as the bad times come, starts to curse and blame circumstances or god."

Sarika said, "Then, We should never be a 'grasshopper'."

I added, "During the good phase, first of all we should be grateful to God and all people who have helped us to achieve this good phase. Many people during riches and success tend to forget God. They forget to thank God. They turn back to God only when these times change. It is important to be with God always at all times, whether good or bad. Do not be selfish by going to god only during bad times. Remember and thank God always.

Ayush added, "Also, we must also be aware of the cycle of time. Like the ant, we must plan for the future, at least economically. While it is very important that we enjoy our lives, the gift of God; we must not be blind to the cycle of time."

Surbhit was quick enough to relate another incident with our discussion. "Do you guys remember our college seniors, Amay Singh and his group?"

Ayush said, "Yeah. Those who got campus placed in big MNCs?"

Surbhit said, "Yes. They got a healthy salary package. They were very joyous. In their first two years of service, they spent all without a second thought, without an investment in their future. Then came the great recession of 2008, and they lost their jobs with no money in account to sustain their flamboyant lifestyle even for a couple of months! I have heard that they are living in a very depressed state, and are not able to accept how life took a quick turn on their fortunes!"

I added, "We can't tame life! We all must understand that. Life cannot be tamed. Period."

Sarika added, "Also, we can't determine whether the impact of a bad phase would be large or small. All we can do is be prepared for it to some extent. It would then act as a buffer and would in turn make a large bad phase into a moderate one. Proper planning like an 'ant' can also make us feel content and happy in a bad time. It is amazing how a small ant can teach the whole humankind such wisdom!"

* * *

Ayush said, "The 'Ant and grasshopper' story could teach us one more thing. During a good phase we must never undermine a person in bad phase. Just because we are having a good phase and someone else is having a low phase, doesn't gives us a reason to undermine him."

I added, "Very well said Ayush. We must remember that the cycle of time would rotate eventually, and we must too face a bad phase in future. We must respect all nonetheless, and only spread love and smiles around."

Sarika said, "A bad phase is a true test of character. First of all, we should not think of a bad time as a punishment or wrath of god in 'our' lives only. Never think that God has chosen you alone for all the burdens, tragedies and grieves in life. This cycle of good and bad times is for all. This bad phase happens to all! All these miseries, hardships and pains are not only for you. Everyone has a fair share of good times as well as bad times.

Secondly, we should not feel envious of a person who is having a good phase. This will only spread hatred in this world. Out of jealousy, this might lead to crimes as well."

Surbhit said thoughtfully, "But many a times, people face such tragedies that their faith in God starts to tremble!"

I said, "Yes. Some tragedies are indeed terrible. They shake the very ground we stand on. They take away our mental peace.

They leave our heart trembling with fear, uncertainty and disbelief! But, always remember that a trembling heart can find solace only in the warmth and love of God! It is love of God, which would help us sail through the tough and tragic times. Always remember that times would change and you are playing a part in God's plan."

The holy saint told me, *'When you are against the tide; when times are not with you, don't get dis-heartened. Challenge yourself'.*

It's just time. It will pass away. God is within us, in our heart. Don't fear of taking the risk; don't fear the challenges of a path. Just take the adverse situation as a challenge, not a punishment. If life is tough to you, you be tougher to be broken. How can you be broken when God is by your side! Go forward, flow through the adverse situation and emerge triumphant. The saint had another beautiful prose on this,

"When you get a reason to cry,
When you get a reason to worry,
When life gives you a grief,
When you encounter a tragedy;
Don't consider it a punishment!

Promise yourself,
To take it as a Challenge!"

Sarika said happily, "That's very inspiring. There is an old saying, 'whatever happens, happens for Good!' This 'good' is for the mankind and we all are playing a part for the betterment of mankind. Consider this cycle of time as test by God. The bad times being our test of character, faith and honesty. The good times bring the benefits of the work we did during our test, the fruits of the seeds that we sowed."

I added, "We should never lose our hope and faith in God. Do not consider bad times as a punishment; consider it as a challenging test. Like a sixth standard kid only gets exam paper made for sixth standard and not the tenth standard; God also gives us difficulties which are solvable as per our own caliber and merit. No difficulty or hindrance in our life is formidable. Remember if this hindrance is yours, then its solution is also in your grasp. You are the sixth standard kid and the exam paper is also for your standard only. Try to solve this test of God!

Just keep the faith and love for God going. Your ship would make through the stormy seas and you would see land soon! May, you always love and confide in the creator, God."

* * *

Sarika said thinking, "I think that it's more of a choice, life! How you see it and live it."

I said, "Very true. The holy saint told me,

'We always have two options in life: to cry or to laugh.'

There is always a choice we can make. Whatever situation life puts us in, there is always a different way to look at it. We can always look at our life, and cry about it or laugh at it."

Sarika said, "When we already know that whatever happens is as per God's plan, then why cry about it!"

Surbhit exclaimed, "But we do have miseries in our lives Sarika!"

I added, "*Life's miseries are how we see it.* It is our persistent thoughts of our miseries that they tend to seem formidable to conquer."

Ayush pitched in, "I read somewhere a wonderful story depicting this. Once there was a comedian. While giving a stand-up performance in front of a hundred people, he told a joke. Almost all people in the theatre laughed.

He narrated the same joke again! The number of people who laughed reduced on hearing the exact same joke. They started wondering as why the comedian is repeating the joke. They found it ridiculous to laugh at the same joke again.

The comedian started again and narrated the same joke again! This time a negligible percentage of people laughed. Some became angrier at the comedian for repeating the joke.

A person stood up and shouted at the comedian, "we want our money back, we haven't come here to listen at same jokes and again. If you don't have anything new then refund our money."

The comedian smiled at the person and said, "Did you all notice what just happened?" The auditorium turned silent now. They knew comedian was trying to narrate more than a joke there.

Comedian said, "The first time I narrated the joke almost every one of you laughed. The next time on hearing the same joke, the percentage of laughter decreased considerably. The third time it was almost nil."

He continued, "*When we laugh only once or twice at a joke which could make us laugh, then why do we go on thinking about a misery over and over again and cry every time! If you can't laugh multiple times over a thing then why do you cry over a thing again and again?*" We let our miseries grow. If you really have to, then cry once and let it go afterwards. It's your choice whether you wish to recall the same misery again and again and keep on crying or not!"

I applauded, "Wow Ayush. What a wonderful story to explain our miseries. Every moment has various angles and perceptions to it. We must train ourselves to look at the sunny and bright side. For an understanding, next time when it rains go out and notice people around. There will always be people who would be trying to not get wet and take a shelter, sometimes even curse the weather for hampering their day plans! You would also notice a few who would be happily walking in the rain; some may be enjoying it with a dance! It's your choice: to curse or to dance. You decide. As we discussed earlier, that it's not worth thinking whether life is fair or not. Just get up and dance, enjoy and live your life."

Sarika said, "I believe that if we start to look for gifts and blessings from God, we will find it wherever we move your eyes. We have been blessed by a beautiful world to live in. Every moment, we must challenge ourselves to look for something around us which would make us feel blessed and happy. We would be amazed! We would have many.

We generally tend to look at our misfortunes, define our lives by our miseries. We tend to look at the gloomy side of any circumstance. One of the main reasons of our sadness is due to our own 'expectations' from people, circumstances or God! The more you expect, chances are that the more you would grieve. *Why give yourself a reason to cry? Why expect more?"*

I added, "Just remember to do your bit. God would bless you with love. From now on, let's focus on our actions and decisions first. We shall try to keep our expectations as low as possible, probably negligible.

When we don't burden ourselves with these expectations, our eyes would be more open to see our blessings. We would start seeing reasons to be happy and grateful for. Now we won't worry about getting drenched in rain. We would go out and enjoy, walk or dance. We would now have made a choice: to laugh."

Ayush shared his views, "Once we are transformed and are able to make the choice of seeing the bright side, we would feel the love of God in life. Earlier, we had blocked this love from entering our lives, by expecting more and more and never being grateful. Now, instead of expecting more, we would enjoy the love in your life, we would be happy and content."

I concluded with a smile, "All we will do now is be happy no matter what the situation is, and spread smiles around. We would do your part in making this world a happier place and make God smile at us. We would become the 'Joy of God'."

* * *

I also wanted to share something important, "Guys, there is something very powerful message which the holy saint taught me. He said,

'Like Attracts Like!'"

Surbhit seemed puzzled, "Didn't we study in physics that opposite poles attract. How come like attracts like?"

I explained further, "That is a physical phenomenon which we had studied in school that opposite attracts. What we are going to understand now is about our thoughts and the power they have in our fate. Even I had the same question for the holy saint and he replied,

'Like thoughts attract like fate.'

The holy saint had explained further that what we think, what we believe in is what we attract in our life!

Simply put, if we think and believe in something, it will manifest! It might take less time or more, but it will. God works in mysterious ways. For some, where this can be good, it can also be bad for someone who is a pessimist. He would always think of bad luck, bad omens and see the negativity in everything. Guess what, he would get more of it! That's what he is attracting, more and more negativity. A pessimist person might not be aware of this law of life. But this still works. His negativity is attracting more negativity around him.

The holy saint told me a mantra to recite whenever I feel sad, dejected, unhappy or negative:

'*If I continue being this way, I would attract more of this in my life.*'"

Sarika shared her views on it, "I recently read a book on this. It talked about the same philosophy. We must always tell ourselves, remind ourselves and check ourselves about what we are thinking. Remember to think good so that you attract good. Always check yourself by asking "What are my thoughts right now, this very moment?" We will get the answer which can tell us what we are attracting right now. And so we get this power to change our thoughts there and then. The power is in our hands, in our brain."

I asked them, "Are you aware of what the side part of our head is called?"

Seeing blank faces I continued, "*Temple*! Co-incidentally 'temple' is the place of worship for various religions. So let's worship our temple, because that's where the real power lies. We just need to understand this power of thoughts and beliefs. When we are able to understand this power, we can truly feel the saying "The power to construct our own fate is in our own hands". We would be able to get what we believed in and we would be happy."

Sarika concluded, "And seeing a happy child always brings smiles on a parent face. So will be the case with God. He would be happy to see his sons and daughters happy and content. May you trust in God's plans and remember that to cry or to laugh is always a choice."

'May, you be the Joy of God'

* * *

Chapter - X

The Final Test: Before God

We left for the airport together to catch our respective flights back home. After check-in, we gathered again to say final good-byes. I checked my watch and we still had half an hour, for discussions!

I said, "Guys, I hope that you will imbibe the 'joy of god' lifestyle and spread it further to your friends and families."

Surbhit said, "Oh man! I should have recorded our discussions. It would have helped me in future."

I said, "Even I didn't record the teaching of the holy saint. This is not a bookish knowledge. The real knowledge is within. Ask your heart sincerely, you will get an answer!

But guys, you need to understand the impact of this lifestyle and then imbibe in yours! It would be better if you would think about our discussions and jot down the important points yourself."

Ayush said happily, "Yeah. That is a great idea. I would go home and take some 'ME' time and think about everything and how I can implement them. It would help and guide me in future."

I said happily, "Before we depart, there is still one aspect which the holy saint taught me. Let's discuss now, we still have some time."

* * *

I continued, "Even the holy saint kept this subject for my last day in Bodh Gaya. After all the teachings, the last day he called me and said that it's a common belief in us that when we die, we either go to heaven or hell. We all have our various thoughts and imaginations on how both worlds would be. Heaven like a paradise is the most beautiful place we could ever imagine. Hell on the other hand is a Devil's den. *But who decides where we go: to God's home or Devil's den?* For a moment, let's not worry about 'who' decides. That is something unknown and not in our control. Let's take care of the part which is in our control, 'Karma'- our actions.

He stated, '*Our actions on this Mother Earth decide 'where' we go!*'"

Sarika said smiling, "and here following the joy of god lifestyle would be our plus point."

I affirmed, "When we aspire to be the 'Joy of God', we do God's work. We would be connected to God. We would always strive to make this world a better place to live in. We would always strive to make it more beautiful, peaceful and full of love. Whether we go to heaven or hell depends on our own 'karma'."

I continued on, "The holy saint that every person should ask himself:

- What have I done to bring smiles to my creator?
- Have I done anything which could have angered or saddened God?

- Do I only think about me, me and me?
- Has my being 'alive' on Mother Earth, benefited the life of even a single needy, poor person?

  Or is it that all I have done is just and only in my best interests?
- Have I ever made another heart cry?
- Has my anger been a problem or created one, for my near and dear ones?
- Has my frustration ever led to any act which could be said to be socially or morally improper?
- The full day that I have lived today, have I done anything to be the 'Joy of God'?

Obviously this list of questions is not comprehensive of all actions and decisions. It's just an example about the type of questions we could always ask ourselves. It shall help us to check ourselves, as in the end God might be considering the same questions in our final test of life."

Ayush said intrigued, "Guys, have you ever wondered about your last moments? During your last moments, what do you want to feel about your own life?"

I added, "When whole life would flashback, would anyone want to fear facing god then? Your life now is full of choices and it's you and you alone, who is responsible for your decisions and actions. Live in such a way today that tomorrow you could proudly say to yourself: "*I have done well. Let's meet my creator now. He shall be happy to see me. I am his masterpiece.*" You would go peacefully and with a smile on your face. Wouldn't you want this for yourself? I would."

Sarika said, "But, to achieve this is not a single task. It's all your life's work. It's all your life's decisions and actions. Each and every day of your life counts. Strive to be 'Joy of God' in each decision or action of yours. Strive to do God's work, help your poor, needy and underprivileged brothers and sisters. 'Morning Mirror Test' and 'ME' time would be great help in our endeavour to take actions or decisions for a greater good. 'Gratitude' would show us the blessings we have received in our life. 'Giving back' would ensure that we think not only about our own self, but also about needy and poor. Checking our bitterness, anger or frustration would prevent us from giving back 'bad' to this world. Remind self that God is one and whatever happens is as per God's plan, just 'believe' in God. The final test before God could be passed daily in small steps."

Ayush asked, "So the methods which we talked about, these are the only way to be the joy of God?"

I answered with a smile, "No my friend. The ideas and methods discussed were those of the holy saint. They will help us in being the joy of God. But these are not the only ways.

Even I asked the same question to the holy saint before leaving. He replied,

> '*Ways and methods could be yours. Look within for knowledge. Look within for answers. Just make sure that you make our mother earth even more beautiful, amazing and lovely! Your creator would smile!*'

The holy saint bid me good-bye with a wonderful poem:

Every light
Would show you a way.
But wind
Might stray you away.

Accept the challenge,
The test of your character
And be righteous.

When times become hard
When roads seem endless
When you feel dejected
Open-up your arms
And let God hug you!

Let God remind you
The love he has for you
That you're God's son
That you're the Joy of God!
'May, you be the Joy of God'

* * *

References

1. https://www.goodreads.com/quotes/202222-if-there-is-righteousness-in-the-heart-there-will-be
2. http://www.goodreads.com/quotes/194973-why-should-a-man-be-moral-because-this-strengthens-his
3. http://www.goodreads.com/quotes/93644-recall-the-face-of-the-poorest-and-weakest-man-you
4. http://www.goodreads.com/quotes/412696-i-have-looked-in-the-mirror-every-morning-and-asked
5. http://www.goodreads.com/quotes/23677-we-know-only-too-well-that-what-we-are-doing
6. http://www.goodreads.com/quotes/11416-the-best-way-to-find-yourself-is-to-lose-yourself
7. http://motivationalreads.com/talk-atleast-day-otherwise-may-miss-meeting-excellent-person-world/
8. theharmonyinstitute.org/ten/ten.pdf